T0110803

The Education of Children Entangled in *Khat* Trade in Ethiopia: The Case of Two *Khat* Market Centers

Girma Negash

Forum for Social Studies (FSS)

Addis Ababa

© 2017 Forum for Social Studies (FSS)

All rights reserved.

Printed in Addis Ababa

FSS Monograph No. 13

ISBN: 978-99944-50-65-7

Forum for Social Studies (FSS)

P.O. Box 25864 code 1000

Addis Ababa, Ethiopia

Email: fss@ethionet.et

Web: www.fssethiopia.org.et

This Monograph has been published with the financial support of the Civil Societies Support Program (CSSP). The contents of the Monograph are the sole responsibilities of the author and can under no circumstances be regarded as reflecting the position of the CSSP or the FSS.

Contents

Acknowledgement

I am grateful to Forum for Social Studies (FSS) and the funding agency, Civil Society Support Program (CSSP), for providing the necessary financial assistance and overall facilitation of the project. I am very much indebted to the entire FSS staff who proved to be supportive throughout this undertaking and especially Dr. Asnake Kefale, Adjunct Researcher at FSS, for his thorough review of the draft monograph and Dr. Zerihun Mohammed for his constant feedback to my thoughts and writing. My appreciation knows no bounds.

I would also like to extend my gratitude to Wondo Genet *Woreda* and Aweday City Administration officials, particularly *Ato* Negatu Girma and *Ato* Nuredin Amin respectively, for rendering invaluable support in identifying local contacts, identifying knowledgeable informants and facilitating the whole research endeavor during my field work in their respective *Woreda*.

I am very much indebted to my informants and participants of the research namely; students, teachers, school-directors, *khat* traders, boys working in the *khat* industry, parents, and civil servants working in the various *Woreda*- level offices for their time and kind collaboration in the process of data collection. My brief contact and cordial relations with them helped me to learn a lot about their daily lives and the nuances of the *khat* business.

My special thanks go to Ato Merkeb Duko who showed personal interest in taking some priceless camera shots of long queues of young boys engaged in their daily routine of carrying *khat* bundles to the *khat* assembling station at Chuko town, Wondo Genet. Those pictures alone speak a lot about the working and living conditions of those boys.

List of Tables

List of Figures

Preface

This study primarily set out to investigate the role of children in *khat* trading activities in the two well-known *khat* marketing centers, Chuko- Wondo Genet and Aweday, in southern and eastern Ethiopia respectively. My knowledge about the *khat* value chain and basic operational principles of *khat* trade in southern Ethiopia goes back to the years 2010 -2014 while I was on a field research in northern Sidama for a PhD dissertation which I finalized and submitted to the Department of History, Addis Ababa University, in 2014.

As a researcher traversing through the *khat* producing countryside of one of the major zones of production for more than half a decade gave me the opportunity to be in constant contact with farmers and traders whose lives are intimately connected with *khat*, and whose hospitalities and insights I lived to appreciate to this day. Then, I observed that some levels of the *khat* value chain have been using the labor of child workers. Nevertheless, such an issue was peripheral to the objective of my dissertation which was aimed at reconstructing the history of economic change in Northern Sidama, located at the northern fringes of the Southern Nations Nationalities Peoples' Region (SNNPR) that spans a period of over half a century since the 1950s.

I had to keep in heart the crude information about the role of children in *khat* trading activities which was later farther invigorated with the curiosity to know what the situation looks like in the other leading *khat* marketing center of the nation- Aweday- in Eastern Hararge, until an opportune moment comes. No other opportune moment could be expected than the year 2015 when Forum for Social Studies (FSS) with the funding secured from Civil Society Support Program (CSSP) envisaged a research project entitled The "Impact of *khat* on Children's Education: A comparative Study of *khat* Producing and Marketing Centers in Southern and Eastern Ethiopia" to which I was designated as a Principal Researcher.

This monograph is the product of that long journey from the inception of the research project all the way through the series of field works and the workshops from which valuable feedbacks have been obtained. It is divided into four chapters. The first chapter is devoted to the background, objectives, methodology and a description of selected study sites. The second chapter is a discussion about theoretical and legal issues pertinent to child labor and employment of children in the context of Africa and Ethiopia. The third chapter presents the main findings of the study chiefly: whether or not children participate in the *khat* marketing activities, the age profile of those children involved in *khat* marketing activities, a survey of the types of jobs those children are engaged in and the work context, a discussion about the working and living conditions of the two categories of children of the *khat* industry namely the 'residents' ' and 'migrants', the impact of involvement in activities related to *khat* marketing on the education of those children who combine schooling and work, and an assessment of possible physical and mental hazards on the child worker. The fourth and final chapter provides important concluding remarks as well as recommendations.

I hope and expect this study will provide some clarity and insight about the way *khat* is being produced and marketed in the major zones of production. It certainly would shade some light on the complexities of the *khat* marketing systems at work in those *khat* marketing and assembling centers which I explored in this work. It will also lift the fog of uncertainties that enshrouded our knowledge and understanding of *khat* related issues such as the role of children and their rights in particular. What I wish urgently and seriously is that this work may bring the issue of child workers engaged in *khat* trading activities, especially the plight of those school - aged working children whom I called 'migrants' to come to the center stage in any event of policy formulation that governs the marketing and consumption of *khat*.

Girma Negash
Addis Abeba
August 2017

1 Introduction

Khat (catha edulis) is an evergreen shrub widely grown and consumed in Ethiopia from as far back as the 14th century, if not earlier. It is documented in the royal chronicle of Amda Seyon (1314-1344 A.D.) that the ruler of the Sultanate of Ifat, Sabradin, had boastfully warned that he will plant *khat* trees at the royal capital of the king. Yemen, in the Arabian Peninsula, is the other country whose name is widely mentioned as a major producer and consumer (Kennedy, 1987: 61; Ezekiel, 2004: 3). *Khat* is also known by several other names such as Chat, Qat, Kat, Quat and Mirra (Kenya). Currently, *khat* cultivation and consumption are no longer confined to Ethiopia and Yemen. They have spread to other parts of Eastern Africa (including Kenya, Uganda and Malawi), and Southern Africa (Zimbabwe, South Africa, Madagascar, Zambia). In the past few decades the consumption of *khat* has gone global. Far off lands, as far east as Australia and New Zealand, as far west as the United States of America, and many countries in Europe have *khat* chewing communities that comprised of both immigrants and a small number of locals (Carrier N., 2007:12;Anderson *et al.*,2007:1).

The earliest known scientific analysis of *khat* varieties and species was made by a Swedish botanist Peter Forsskal in his work *Flora-Aegypto-Arabica* in 1975, hence the reference *Catha edulis Forsskal* (Kennedy, 1987:177; Ezekiel, 2004: 14). Studies on the pharmacology of *khat* reveal that the leaves of this plant contain psychoactive substances capable of stimulating the central nervous system and creating temporary euphoria. Among others, the most active ingredients in *khat* are the alkaloids cathinone and cathine (also known as norpseudoephedrine) and norephedrine (Kalix,1992; Al-hebshi and Skaug, 2005; WHO 34th Report, 2006:10). In spite of the range of psychological, physiological and economic adverse effects that *khat* consumption supposedly[1] causes, different social groups chew *khat* leaves and its tender twigs for various reasons. Some chew *khat* for pleasure and recreation, some to get 'high' or stimulated. Some others claim that *khat* has the potency to repel sleep and fatigue. Others believe that it is an herbal medicine against common cold, dysentery and a range of other diseases. In some Ethiopian cultures *khat* plays an important role in social events such as weddings,

---

[1] "Supposedly" because, although significant progress has been made, *khat* research at present is still at its infancy and findings about its health effects are inconsistent and less conclusive. For some, even those reported as *khat*-caused health problems are "exaggerated." See (Kennedy, 1987: 231; Ezekiel, 2008: 787-788).

funerals, and reception of guests. Some Muslims also believe that they chew *khat* for a religious purpose (Anderson *et al.*,2007:3-5; Ezekiel,2004:11).

Khat got international attention since the second half of the 20th century. In 1964, the Economic and Social Council of the UN passed a resolution (XXXVII/1964/1025) that pronounced *khat* chewing is a cause of "grave social problems." However, *khat* was not included in the list of "controlled" substances, in the 2003 report filed by WHO Expert Committee. In its 34th report, the WHO Expert Committee on Drug Dependence reviewed available data on *khat* and decided that it should not be a controlled substance. Despite recognizing the alleged social and health problems that excessive use of *khat* might cause, the Committee did not recommend the scheduling of *khat*. The Committee rather made a suggestion that those adverse effects could be overcome through educative campaigns (WHO 34th Report, 2006:11).

There is inconsistency in the legal status of *khat* in different countries. *Khat* use is legal in Yemen, Kenya, and Uganda. Only recently European policy towards *khat* showed a major shift. For example, the Netherlands, which was a distribution center for suppliers from other European countries such as Germany and Sweden, introduced legislation that banned the trade and possession of *khat* in January 2012. Heathrow, the main British airport, had been a hub for redistribution in Europe until a new law that has banned *khat* came into force in June 2014. *Khat* is illegal and banned in Saudi Arabia, Sweden, Canada, Finland, France, Jordan and Tanzania. In the USA, it is a "controlled" substance, the consumption of which is illegal.

In Ethiopia, as it stands today, there is no national policy regarding *khat* production and use. In recent years, *khat* cultivation has been expanding aggressively to regions formerly known for their cereal and coffee production. Even more so, the habit of *khat* chewing is expanding at an alarming rate among different social groups irrespective of gender, age, religion and ethnic background. An issue of concern to all has become the fact that young college students, high school students and unemployed youth in and around urban areas are being increasingly attracted to the habit of *khat* chewing (Girma, 2007 E.C).

On the other hand, *khat* has already assumed the position of becoming one of the leading foreign currency earners for the country. The revenue regional and federal governments are generating from *khat* trade, and employment opportunities the *khat* industry has created are so vivid and self-evident that they can hardly be underestimated. Few will also dispute the economic benefits that *khat* farming has brought to farmers. For example, in Hararge, the high cash return has increased the income of farming communities, which has allowed them to satisfy their basic needs with much more ease (Ezekiel, 2008; Kingele, 1998).

Owing to the burgeoning demand from the national and international markets over the past decades, *khat* production and trade has evolved tremendously with conspicuous changes on techniques of production and marketing all along the value chain from the farm gate to the various centers of distribution. Year after year more and more farmlands have been allocated for *khat* agriculture; indigenous technologies were improvised with the evident effect of maximized yield. The system of *khat* marketing, especially the way the commodity has been mobilized, assembled, and transported over the last several decades, has also evolved through time in such a way that it has adopted some of the basic principles that typify a modern commercial undertaking. Ultimately *khat* production and trade has grown to assume a cash crop proportion in most of the zones of production (Girma, 2014).

1.1 Research Objectives

In this study, an attempt has been made to examine the causes and consequences of the involvement and active participation of young people in *khat* marketing and trade at different stages of the *khat* value chain. Among the range of other consequences, arguably the most undesired could be the one unwittingly ruining the education and overall intellectual development of those children who are directly participating in *khat* trading activities. Lured by 'easy money', a good part of those working-children are believed to have given up school because they left their parents and villages in pursuit of the presumed fortune believed to exist at one or the other *khat* marketing centers. A few others had to dropout from school unable to continue as 'part-time students' under the unbearable circumstances and working environment in the *khat* industry. A general trend observed among those school-age children working in the *khat* industry is the propensity of missing classes and schooldays as a whole. Even those who have managed to go to school and attend classes are under enormous pressure and challenges in pursuing their education effectively.

Moreover, it is highly likely that these young workers who are active participants in the trading and marketing of *khat* could be subjected to some of the concomitant effects, or "occupational hazards," so to speak, caused by the work of which they are an integral part. One such hazard is the habit of regular *khat* chewing and "dependence" on *khat* at a tender age. Once again, one of the most obvious adverse effects of any "addiction"/ "dependence" is the education of the person involved. What have been widely articulated so far in the literature are the indirect consequences of "addiction"/ "dependence" on children born from "addicted" parents and the family at large (Yeshigeta & Abraham, 2004: 180;Beckerleg,2006:233; Green, 1999: 41). On the other hand, evidence from some recent studies shows that children who are in their teens are active participants in *khat* trading activities in some of the known production zones (Girma 2014). A possible scenario that can be drawn from such an active involvement would be that those children might well pick up a *khat* chewing habit.

On account of the fact that the target population of this study are children in their school- age, the central issue would be addressing the impact of their involvement in the *khat* industry on their education and academic performance. It is therefore envisaged to identify the nature and magnitude of those adverse effects caused by involvement in *khat* trade and to come up with insights that would inform future policy. It is also hoped that findings from this research would shed more light on the issue and help to develop pathways for intervention by governmental agencies and non-governmental actors, including Civil Society Organizations (CSOs), community based organizations, parents and the community at large.

The research has the following specific objectives:

- identify the prominent factors behind children's involvement in *khat* trading activities;

- identify how involvement in the *khat* business adversely affects the education of children and / or vulnerable youth in the zones of *khat* production;

- investigate how working in the *khat* industry in the selected research sites and their environs affect children's school enrollment, attrition, effectiveness, and overall engagement ;

- assess the level of intervention so far, if there is any, to contain the problem by governmental and non-governmental actors;

- Investigate the existing legal framework to protect the right of the working children and its effectiveness to address the problem; and

- Identify pathways (policy reforms) and options for intervention by governmental and non-governmental CSOs to mitigate the problem and address the needs of child.

1.2   Methods and Approaches

1.2.1   Research Design

The research design I have employed in this study is what has come to be known as the mixed method. This is a relatively recent approach that involves collecting, combining and analyzing both forms of data, the qualitative and quantitative, in just one single study (Johnson *et al.*, 2007,119). One of the rationales for using this approach is the fact that the use of multiple data sources would broaden the chance of triangulation of data. It also helps to neutralize some of the limitations inherent to the two classical methods of inquiry. The mixed method approach gives the opportunity to employ data garnered from one particular source to inform, complement, or compensate the other (Creswell, 2003: 15).

The attempt to understand experiences, perspectives and thoughts of participants through the qualitative methods of inquiry was best articulated and triangulated using quantitative data. In my case, the fact that both forms of data have been collected simultaneously the "concurrent procedure" of data analysis was adopted as an ideal procedure for integrating information from both methods for interpretation and analysis. Practically, the quantitative data have been used as an indicator of trends and patterns.

1.2.2   Target Population and Participants

The target population of this study are children working in the *khat* industry, in different capacities, at two well-known *khat* marketing centers, Aweday and Wondo Genet in eastern and southern Ethiopia respectively. The participants of this study are young workers taking part in the complex trading activities at the different stages of the *khat* value chain. Some of these children work at the farm gates, some at market places and some in the "*khat* workshops." The word child used in this study, unless expressed otherwise, refers to children below the age of

18 in line with the 1989 UN Convention on the Rights of the Child (Art. 2) which defines a child as "every human being below the age of 18 years."

Preliminary observations show that the target group of this study are of two major groups. The first group consists of local boys who are still living with their parents but deeply involved in the process of *khat* marketing. In this study, they are referred to as "residents." The other group of the study population are those who came from other nearby *Warada*[2] and Peasant Associations seeking employment in the above- mentioned *khat* markets. These ones I called, for lack of a better term, 'migrants'. What the two groups have in common is that both are school-age children who are supposed to spend much of their time in schools, and at the same time involved in activities related to *khat* trade. The difference between the two is that members of the first group are living with their parents with some degree of family control and /or support, while the latter have none of these privileges.

1.2.3 Sample and Sampling Procedure: Selecting Participants

The situation on the ground made it difficult to have an accurate estimate of the number of child workers in the two study sites. Lack of any official, or unofficial, list of children working in the *khat* industry and the difficulty of getting access to them seriously hampered the effort to have a sampling frame that would allow to get the subset of the larger population under study. For this reason, I have adopted the purposive sampling technique. Accordingly, selection of participants for questionnaires and interviews was made through contacting available members of the target group.

Therefore, all the participants who filled the questionnaires for the survey were boys under the age of 18 who are workers in the *khat* industry at different capacities. Yet, the major challenge remained to be the creation of sampling population. However, the validity of the sample was increased by trying to approximate random selection, and by reducing as many sources of bias as possible. In consultation with local officials and teachers, we have identified schools in which most members of the target population are enrolled. In Chuko town, there are two high schools and one elementary and junior high school, named, Wondo Genet Secondary and Preparatory School, and Wondo Genet Secondary School;

---

[2] The lowest-level administrative unit in Ethiopia since the imperial period which is roughly equivalent to a sub- district.

and one Chuko Elementary and Junior High School. Local officials and teachers estimated that there would be about 60 students who work in the *khat* industry in each of the three schools I have chosen 20 participants from each school, which would make a total of sixty student-*khat* workers to represent the group whom I called "residents."

In Aweday too, schools have been my focal areas for data collection. I have used three schools: one high school (Aweday Preparatory and Secondary School) and two elementary schools namely; Aweday Elementary School and *Fendisha* Elementary School where the majority of the young boys working in the *khat* industry are enrolled and attend classes. Here, I had to use availability sampling and a total of 30 students who are all residents and school-goers were selected to fill the questionnaire.

As far as the 'migrants' are concerned, I have to rely on availability sampling by using children of this category with whom I managed to get in touch. They might be many in number but they are disinterested and resistant meeting unknown people for fear of being sent home hence elude any contact with others. I, however, managed to get the participation of 20 children of this group. Nine other 'migrants' have also filled the questionnaire because, although they are 'migrants', they are still able to pursue their education defying all the challenges. This raised the total number of 'migrants' to 29.

1.2.4 Data Collection Instruments

The most outstanding qualitative data gathering instruments used to generate data for this research were in-depth interviews and focus group discussions (FGD). I have engaged as many children, both 'migrants' and residents, as possible. Interviews and discussions with teachers, parents, *khat* traders and local authorities helped me to establish contact with groups who have a very keen concern with the subject of study. Observation and secondary sources of data from schools, such as rosters, attendance sheet and report cards were other means of extracting qualitative data. The quantitative data used in this research was extracted through a questionnaire filled by a sample population of 90 participants selected in the two study sites. Respondents who filled the questionnaire in Wondo Genet comprise of both "resident" school-going children and 'migrants'. In Aweday, however, all the respondents are "resident" school-going children working in the *khat* industry. The data collected through the various tools of data gathering has been transcribed and qualitatively analyzed using a thematic approach.

1.2.5   Data Collection Procedure

All types of empirical data for this research have been collected through two-rounds of fieldwork in the two selected study sites. The first round fieldwork was conducted from November 9 - December 6, 2015 in Chuko town (the administrative headquarter of Wondo Genet *Warada* on the northern fringes of Sidama Zone) where the Tafara *khat* market is situated. The data collection process here was more intense and rigorous than anticipated earlier because of the fact that 60 out of the total of 90 questionnaires for the survey had to be filled by study participants here. Secondly, I considered the presence of 'migrant' child workers in large numbers, more visible as a separate group, engaged in distinctly known work types as an opportunity to make an exhaustive investigation of their role in the *khat* industry and their working and living conditions. The second round fieldwork was conducted in the other study site, the town of Aweday, in Eastern Hararge, from January 5- 18, 2016. Here, although young persons both from Aweday and those who came from other areas are found to be active participants in the process of *khat* marketing, the 'migrants' do not make up a substantively distinct group engaged exclusively in *khat* trading activities. Their jobs are not limited to *khat* trade and some of them, even though they are 'migrants' they may not come to the *Magala Jimaa* as long as they get something to do for a living outside the *khat* market. Therefore, not withstanding their presence in the town, it was not easy to identify and contact them as a separate group so as to fill the questionnaire. Therefore, the collection of primary data through questionnaires and in-depth interviews was conducted in the schools mentioned above by approaching resident school-going boys working at the *Magala Jimaa*.

1.3   Description of the Study Sites

1.3.1   Chuko Town and the Tafara Market

The *Tafara* market is the largest *khat* market in northern Sidama. Arguably, along with Aweday in East Hararge, it is one of the two largest *khat* assembling centers in the entire country. This southern *khat* marketing center is found in Chuko town, formerly known as Basha, located 23.5 kilometers to the northeast of the town of Hawaasa, and 272 kilometers to the south of Addis Ababa. Following the administrative restructuring adopted in 2005, the town of Chuko became the administrative capital of Wondo Genet *Warada* in Sidama Zone. It was then Basha town was renamed Chuko.[3]

As regards to its present size and economic importance, Chuko town owes much to *khat* trade. Even if *khat* trade was not the reason for the birth of the town, it is the reason behind its present status and economic significance. A keen observer some three decades ago has the following to say regarding the impact of *khat* trade on the future of the town; "This *khat* town grew from a small village in the late 1980s …when it became the major *khat* wholesale market in Wondo Genet" (Gessesse, 2007: 13). The nearly threefold dramatic rise of the population of Chuko from 7000 in the late 1980s to 18,467 (2007 Population and Housing Census of Ethiopia: Statistical Report for SNNPR: 1132, Table 1A), in 2007 is an important indicator about the significance of the thriving *khat* trade to the town.

A fateful development in the transformation of Chuko into a town of conspicuous size was the fast growing *khat* trade in northern Sidama, especially since the late 1980s. The historic town of Kella, some six kilometers to the north of the then Basha, preceded the town of Basha as a *khat* trading center. Kella, situated on a long-distance trade route at about the turn of the 20[th]century, happened to be a major customs gate for *Dajjazmach* Balcha[4] from about the 1890s hence the name Kella which means customs post. Various other locations within the town of Basha as it was known in those days served as centers of *khat* transaction up until the closing years of the 1980s. The year 1988 was a landmark in the emergence of the *Tafara khat* market in this same town.

The *Tafara* market is situated some 600 meters from the main road that bisects the town of Chuko. It is only 7-8 minutes walking distance to the east of the road. Gauged by all standards, chiefly by the quantity of the *khat* daily transported out of *Tafara*, it stands as the largest *khat* market in southern Ethiopia. No other *khat* market in southern Ethiopia is ever known to deliver ten fully- loaded Isuzu trucks[5] on average every day. If Aweday, as described by the authors of *The Khat Controversy*, is "…the hub for the eastern Ethiopian *khat* trade," (Anderson et al.,

---

[3] For other details of origin and historical evolution of Basha town, see Girma Negash (2014) "Agriculture and Trade in Northern Sidama Since 1950: A History." (PhD Dissertation, Department of History, AAU.)

[4] The governor of the former Sidamo Governorate - General, later Province, since 1896 for a total of over twenty- seven years divided into three separate blocks with some interruption between each of them.

[5] Each Isuzu truck roughly carries up to 3,000 Kilograms of *khat* at once.

2007: 45) so is *Tafara* for the *khat* trade in southern Ethiopia without any other serious contender.

Overlooking the *Tafara* market, there is a small hill- top to the north-west, which recently has undergone an exemplary scheme of aforestation. Of a very high practical value is the great number of small houses (which I call "*khat* workshops") that have proliferated surrounding the market, built by private individuals. They are rented to *khat* traders who need them to do all the packaging of *khat* before its departure to different destinations. In front of the main gate, are several shops and tearooms providing a wide range of services to customers frequenting the market. A very interesting tradition observed by all frequenting the *Tafara* market was the tradition of "Whistle Blowing," that takes place every day at 6:00 p.m., to mark the official beginning of market operation at *Tafara*.[6]

1.3.2 Aweday and its Magala Jimaa

The other major *khat* assembling center in Ethiopia to which I made an earlier reference citing the *The Khat Controversy* (2007) is the *Magala Jimaa* (the *khat* market) of the town of Aweday, in Eastern Hararge, Oromia Regional State. Aweday and its *khat* market which is locally known as *Magala Jimaa* are swarmed by multitudes of *khat* traders and suppliers every day from mid-day all the way through to the next morning.

Informants recall that initially *khat* trade in Aweday was a disorganized roadside business without a specific center at a specific place. It was not a full-time occupation of professional traders exclusively engaged in *khat* trade. It was the establishment of the *Magala Jimaa*, in 1973, with stalls for the marketeers to

---

[6] During the span of time between my two fieldworks in the region from January 2012 to December 2015, the *Tafara* market, for good or bad, has undergone significant transformation both in terms of physical appearance and mode of transaction.. Along with the establishment of the "Wondo Genet *khat* Trading Share Company in 2013, a new arrangement was introduced that abolished the key role of individual entrepreneurs locally known as "*Kontractors*." These were handful of men with better capital in charge of transporting *khat* bought from Tafara market to various destinations paying all dues at customs posts along the way in return for collecting what was due to them from *khat* traders at the receiving end. At present, with a renovation project well underway, the Tafara market has been totally demolished. Its former stalls have been totally cleared leaving the place for concrete-walled spacious rooms still under construction. Gone with the good old days was the tradition of "whistle blowing." As a result of the changes on the *khat* market "whistle blowing" is no longer practiced to mark the beginning of market operations, as I have observed the market scene and operation once again in December 2015.

stay at and make price negotiations that brought some degree of order to *khat* trade. Although the *Magala Jimaa* is the epicenter of Aweday's *khat* business, nowadays *khat* trading activities have already overtaken the entire town and no part of the town is left intact. This may be the reason why many people refer to Aweday itself as just a *khat* market rather than a town in its own right.

Aweday is located about 12 kilometers to the south-west of the historic town of Harar, and 370 kilometers to the east of Addis Ababa. It is located at 2036 meters above sea level and has a *Woinadega* climate. The population of Aweday in 2007 was estimated to be over 48,680 (Aweday Town Administration: 2014).

According to local traditions, the town of Aweday was founded sometime around 1954. Historically, the site where the present town of Aweday had been located was a small village known as Diddimtu (which literally means "the reds").[7] The early impetus for the scattered village to grow into a sizable settlement came from the long distance trade from Harar to the fast growing town of Dire Dawa that crossed Diddimtu. At about 1954a certain local elder named Sheikh Yusuf, realizing the business potential of the locality, built the first house to be rented for coffee and tea sellers. By about 1960 the number of small houses constructed at the site had already reached eighteen. Another contributory factor for Aweday to surpass all other competing *khat* markets in the region was the establishment of a military camp at Hammarresa, very close to Harar, in 1964. The town of Hammarresa, which managed to get some degree of prominence at that time, was heavily populated by a large number of men- in- uniforms who were not allowed to chew *khat*. Consequently, the heated *khat* trading activity at Hammarresa started to decline. The nearby Aweday, along the Addis Ababa-Dire Dawa road, looked a more convenient alternative for *khat* traders to establish a new center at (Aweday Town Administration, 2014).

From such a beginning, in a little over half a century, Aweday grew to become a vibrant *khat* trading center where tons of *khat* from the farmlands of East and West Hararge region are sorted, graded and packed for domestic and international shipment. According to the Aweday City Administration, in 2015some 60,000-

---

[7] Still another tradition maintains that the town of Aweday draws its name from the burial ground of a local spiritual person called Weday who passed away around 1928 and buried at the same place where he used to teach about fairness and justice. The site of burial was widely known as *Awala-Weday* which in local language means the burial of Weday. It was *Awala-Weday* whichgradually evolved to be pronounced as Aweday (Aweday Town Administration (2014) A brochure titled "The Foundation of Aweday and its Overall Features").

80,000 kilograms of *khat* were brought to the *khat* market at Aweday every day, carried by a variety of means of transport, chiefly Isuzu trucks. Presently, *khat* trade is a means of livelihood for about 10,000 inhabitants of the town whose lives are connected to *khat* trade in one or another way.[8] Some 8,000 *khat* farmers, women and men alike, are regular visitors to the town to sell their *khat* bundles. Thanks to *khat* trade, the daily capital turnover of Aweday town amounts to 10 million birr (Aweday Town Administration, 2015).

Khat trade beyond a mere economic activity is the reason for Aweday to earn the epithet "the only town in Ethiopia where the sun never sets." The hustle and bustle of the day's business at Aweday begins at the dawn of the day almost every day and continues to the night. The non-stop trading activity in the town is the reason for 24 hours-round banking service at the town which makes the city unique in the country. Other services like the "door-less shops" also function for almost 24 hours.

---

[8] It is estimated that not less than a quarter of this number are youth in their teens.

2 Theoretical Considerations and Legal Perspectives

2.1 Is "Work Free Childhood" Feasible in Africa?

To start with, not all kinds of work, or conditions of work, in which children are involved are child labor. Definitions of childhood, child labor and children's work should be understood and conceptualized against the background of the widely varied cultural and social contexts that shaped the child's experiences, aspirations and expected roles to play. Of all other discourses so far dominant in the literature, the 'socially constructed child' that prescribes the meaning and value societies attach to children as socially and culturally constructed, and vary from culture to culture and from one society to another seems to be well grounded (Nsamenang, 2008:213; Kjørholt, 2004: 20-21). For instance, in the Western cultures it is widely believed that children are beings moving towards autonomy; while in many African cultures they are understood as instruments of lineage continuity, and often as 'wealth in people' that entails the obligation of supporting family and provision of labor in their capacity (Ansell, 2005:65).

There are divergent sometimes contentious definitions and analysis in the discourse about child labor. Those differing views about the issue of child labor are anchored on two overarching perspectives. The first one is the frame of thinking that perceives children as independent and competent economic and social actors as opposed to the other notion that recognizes children as dependents and vulnerable. In the first group are those who believe that children's involvement in work is not harmful as such and rather should be accepted as normal. Protagonists of this view argue that children should participate in production as well as consumption. Their participation in work is not an inhibition but rather an empowerment. It is rather an informal school which would allow children to learn the basics of discipline, work ethic and life skills that are useful assets for the future (Nsamenang 2008: 216; Bourdillon 2000). Those scholars who emphasize the merits of children's participation in work claim that disallowing children from participation in production and consumption is an act of dis-empowering them and would ultimately add to their dependence and vulnerability (Rwezaura 1998; Bourdillon 2000). They also reinforce their argument saying that most working children when asked their desire if they want to continue working, their answer is in the affirmative. Therefore, it is a matter of right for these children to be able to express their opinions and wishes on the basis of Article 12 of "Convention on the Rights of the Child" (CRC) - that is 'the right to express an opinion.'

The other line of thinking espoused by an equally good number of scholars is that children should be able to enjoy a work- free childhood. Scholars of this group argue that work at an early age adversely affects the physical, emotional and intellectual development of a child. The child worker is more exposed to injuries and other health hazards than the adult. Children are not able to foresee the eventual harms and latent risks intrinsic to some occupations (Assefa and Boyden 1988:3-4; Kassouf et al.,2001:21). Moreover, in any market system operating in line with capitalist principles profit and exploitation is involved which would never leave children intact. It is to be noted that working children, more often than not, are less paid than their adult counterparts. Child labor is also referred to as a 'labor without representation.' There are no trade unions or rights groups to protect the rights of the working child from long working hours and negotiate a better working condition and payment. A weaker bargaining power gives extra advantage to employers to fire children without compensation any time they want. The conclusion is that making profit out of the labor of, and through the exploitation of, mentally immature and physically frail children is reprehensible (Assefa and Boyden, 1988: 7; Bourdillon, 2000). Last but not least, a more glaring casualty when children are set to be involved in paid work is their access to formal education and their performance in school. Taking part in any kind of productive endeavor undoubtedly shares the time which children are supposed to spend on education and leisure. Owing to the expansion of schools and school systems organized on shift basis (as has been the case in Ethiopia for a long time to date),there is a wider opportunity for children to combine work and schooling. Nevertheless it has become increasingly evident that combining paid work and schooling jeopardizes the academic performance of those children involved.(Bourdillon and Boyden, J., 2014: 13-14; Tizita, 2010:81-82).

In Africa and most other 'Third World' countries the economic realities as well as the social and cultural milieu hardly allow work to be an adult preserve. According to Nsamenang (2008; 216), for most African cultures "child work is not abusive, but an African mode of social integration and responsibility training." These cultures do not allow children to sit idle and be dependent on their parents. Many children across the continent are engaged in different forms of work. The context in which children work may vary from culture to culture and from one agro-ecological zone to another. In a nut shell, the very idea of child labor originated in the western world with factory work and is irrelevant to Africa (Nieuwenhuys, 1998: 238).

Researchers have identified three distinct categories of work occupied by the child worker namely; work in the informal sector, in the formal sector and in the family (referring to family-run business or farming). In rural Africa household chores and looking after livestock is the exclusive domain of the rural child. In African peasant economies the family is the unit of production where individual households are labor self – sufficient and children are supposed to contribute to the labor capital of the family. These things they do, in large measure, as their cultural responsibility to support the family and usually unpaid (Ansell,2005:70, 161- 163; Katz,2004: 143).

The pervasive influence of global capitalism and the introduction of cash crop agriculture in many African economies gave a new impetus for the intensification of the role of the child in economically productive activities. This state of affairs impacted the existing livelihood trajectories and the situation of children "working for others" in return for wages became a normative economic practice (Abebe & Kjørholt, 2009:176). But as time rolled on, families and children themselves were obsessed with these kinds of work, at times closing their eyes to the possible damage such work might cause on the health, education and the future of the child in general. Many African countries, as a clear endorsement of children's work, at different stages of their history, went to the extent of adopting a national policy that combined education with productive work (Bourdillon, 2006:1).

With the intensification of a *khat*-based commercial agriculture in both the two study sites, a major shift has taken shape bringing working children to the center of the fast growing *khat* industry. In those areas where the majority of people earn their livelihood from *khat* production and marketing, for many young people, developmental progress would become a continuity of experience from a part-time student and child worker to a full time youth/adult *khat* trader.

2.2 Working Children in Ethiopia: An Inquiry into the Socio-legal Landscape

"The right of the child to be protected from economic exploitation and from performing any work that is likely to be hazardous or to interfere with the child's education, or to be harmful to the child's health or physical, mental, spiritual, moral or social development."

Article 32 of the Convention on the Rights of the Child (CRC) adopted by the United Nations General Assembly on 20 November 1989,(United Nations 1989)

The rapid industrialization of the Western world since the mid-19th century and the rampancy and harsh treatment of the child worker heightened the debate and increased the concern about child labor. This led to the various legislations issued at different times aimed at the abolition/elimination of child labor and the exploitation of children. Anti- child labor legislations of the early days recognized child labor more broadly as "waged work undertaken by a child under a certain age." Right from those early times, however, authorities are divided between those considered immoral and exploitative forms of children's work and a broad spectrum of other 'less harmful' activities such as housekeeping, child minding, and running errands. The latter are tolerated and even sanctioned by many governments and on the grounds of their socializing and training effects to the child's future (Nieuwenhuys,1998: 238-239; Ansell, 2005:175).

Despite the long- standing debate whether children should work or not the fact remains that a good number of children all across the globe continue to take part in diverse productive and/or non-productive (household–related) activities. Some children are engaged in paid work and some work in their households without payment. The domestic and often unpaid labor of children revolve around supporting their families in such activities as to taking care of siblings, running errands, collecting firewood, house cleaning and assisting in farming and tending herds. On the other hand, an overwhelming number of children are also engaged in paid work that helps them to generate a sizable income. Leaving aside the worst forms of child labor such as slavery, debt bondage, child trafficking and prostitution, normally children in different parts of the world provide paid labor services as porters, vendors, domestic servants, shoe shiners, tea and coffee pickers and even as miners in some cases (Bourdillon, 2000).

According to one study, the Ethiopian countryside has a higher prevalence of "child labor" than the urban centers with the ratio of 86.6% to 77.9%. The study also reports that most working children are engaged in non-economic activities and children work with no financial remuneration (Ghetnet, 2010:16). In addition to domestic work, other activities working children in rural areas undertake include animal herding, collecting firewood, and grass-cutting, fetching water, sweeping the floor, making coffee and washing cloths. In terms of gender, girls outnumber boys in these activities. However, this should not be conjectured to mean that urban children in Ethiopia are work free. Recent studies demonstrate that the phenomenon of "child labor" in Ethiopian towns and cities is increasingly on the rise. The commonest of jobs outside the realm of the household taken by children in urban areas include, among others; shoe shining, assistants on mini-bus taxis the *woyala*, [as they are known in Addis], lottery ticket selling, petty trade and running errands. Not included in this list are prostitution and weaving which involve exploitation and child abuse of various forms (Abebe & Kjørholt, 2009:181; Ghetnet, 2010:17).

In spite of the existence of both child labor and working children in different capacities, both in the countryside and urban centers, Ethiopia is not yet able to adopt a comprehensive legal document to regulate and protect the rights of its working children. However, the FDRE Constitution, the Civil and the Criminal Code and the Revised Family Law address child right issues. For instance, the federal Constitution sounds clear and unequivocal in protecting and safeguarding children. Art.36 (1d) stipulates that "Every child has the right: not to be subject to exploitative practices, neither to be required nor permitted to perform work which may be hazardous or harmful to his or her education, health or well-being." Similarly, the 2005 Criminal Code adopted some stringent provisions criminalizing acts that in any way encroach into the well-being of the child in some of its articles. Art. 525 (b) of this code prohibits children's involvement in the production and trafficking of drugs; and Art. 596(3) outlaw enslaving children. Trafficking minors aimed at compulsory labor has also been made illegal by Art.597 (1). A Few of the protective provisions adopted by the Labor Proclamation No. 377/2003 include that the minimum age for employment is 14, and set that the maximum number of hours children should work must not exceed 7 hours a day. The Revised Family Code of FDRE (2000) also touches upon some important aspects of child rights. For instance, Art.195 stipulates the revocation of adoption, "where the adopter, instead of looking after the adopted child as his own child, handles him as a slave, or in conditions resembling slavery, or makes him engage in immoral acts for his gain, or handles him in any other manner that is detrimental to his future."

Those efforts at national level aimed at protecting the rights of the child have also been buttressed by Ethiopia's ratification of international instruments, chiefly the ILO and United Nations conventions. Ethiopia's ratification of two United Nations Conventions/Protocols and two ILO Conventions on different occasions could be considered as substantive measures in response to the call for the protection of the rights of the child. Those international Conventions are the United Nations Convention on the Rights of the Child of 1989 (UN-CRC) and

"The Protocol to Prevent, Suppress and Punish Trafficking in Persons, Especially Women and Children (Palermo Protocol, 2000).

If we focus on ILO's Minimum Age Convention, 1973(No.138) and Worst Forms of Child Labor, 1999 (No. 182) ratified by Ethiopia, we will find out that some provisions in the country's national legislations have been introduced in order to address some of the mandatory provisions of the ILO. For instance, in response to Convention No. 138, the 2003 Ethiopian Labor Proclamation (No. 377) fixed the age of 14 as a minimum age for employment (Art.89, 2).With full endorsement of international standards, the Labor Law has also prohibited 'young persons' from taking part in any 'hazardous work.' Except that our focus is on matters related to child labor, the two important provisions in the Revised Family Law of Ethiopia - the mandatory birth registration for every child and the provision that obliges the government to put in place structures/institutions that would execute the process and keep the records - is in part a progress in the direction of improving the right of the child. Yet again there remained plenty of challenges to the issue of child labor. Arguably the condition of those children working in the "*khat* workshops" for long hours, often at night, owing to the requirements of *khat* business, risking their education and their physical and psychological well-being is highly precarious.

The fact that the term child labor is loosely used in the current discourse and literature calls for a working definition at this juncture in order to show how it should be understood in this study. More often than not, the term "child labor" is interchangeably used with other more legal and less harmful engagements of the child. ILO's Statistical Information and Monitoring Program on Child Labor (SIMPOC) considers lots of variables; such as the age range of the children involved and the number of hours they are engaged in work per week, before making a decision whether or not a child labor situation exists.

One has to make sure the prevalence of all these conditions [9] and measure the scale of their impact on the child before making a pronouncement about the existence of child labor.

---

[9] Here is SIMPOC's elaborate set of criterion that are used to determine the existence of a child labor situation; i) a child under 12 who is economically active for one or more hours per week; (ii) a child 14 and under who is economically active for at least 14 hours per week; (iii) a child 17 and under who is economically active for at least 43 hours per week; (iv) a child 17 and under who participates in activities that are "*hazardous by nature or circumstance*" for one or more hours per week; and, (v) a child 17 and under who participates in an "*unconditional worst form of child*

Others also use a less complex yardstick to determine whether or not a condition of child labor exists which hangs on three key considerations: "the child's age, the type and conditions of work, and the effects of the work on the child." In contrast to child labor, the term "children's work," frequently appears in the literature and looks more broad and overarching. It refers to the wide range of activities performed by children; be it paid or unpaid work, domestic work or market-oriented activities, full time or part- time, in the formal or informal sector, in a family business or in an enterprise owned by another employer. The act of child labor might take place in one of the above listed contexts, thus it should be viewed as a subset of the broader designation, children's work (Ghetnet, 2010:13).

Indeed, what is happening in the two *khat* marketing centers under study has a stark resemblance with what the ILO defines as child labor "… work that is deemed inappropriate because the workers are too young, or because *it has adverse impact on their well-being or education,* [emphasis added] or is considered hazardous"(Ansell, 2005:160).The empirical data and my own observation show that the above ILO parameter is more or less fulfilled to claim that child labor is in existence in the two study sites. However, I preferred, in this work, to explaining the situation in terms of children's work rather than "child labor."I argue in this study that the on-going *khat* trade in the study areas is making use of labor provided by children who are "too young," and whose education and well-being would be adversely affected in one way or another. The study has also underlines that these children are involved in the trade of a psychoactive substance capable of causing addiction. This makes the whole affair more complex and morally reprehensible for a nation to stay indifferent while a sizable number of its school-age children do not go to school and are plunged into addiction at a very young age.

---

labor" such as trafficked children, children in bondage or forced labor, armed conflict, prostitution, pornography, illicit activities. (ILO, Defining Child labor: A Review of the Definitions of Child Labor in Policy Research, 2009: 19).

3 The Interface between Children's Involvement in *Khat* Trading Activities and their Education

3.1 The Age Profile of Child Workers in the *Khat* Industry

It is difficult to provide the precise number of children engaged in activities related to preparing *khat* bundles before they leave the production zones. Local officials and veteran *khat* traders prefer talking in terms of percentages than giving a near accurate estimate. Note that *khat* trade is full of irregularities and inconsistent practices. For instance, the number of people involved in the trade is not consistent all through a given year, or even in a given month. Traders might go out of business due to a strained *khat* supply in some seasons, or shortage of capital, or even bankruptcy. Moreover, people can easily turn to other more sustainable businesses whenever they wish to. Most importantly, children, especially the 'migrants' as in Aweday, may be forced to turn to any of the available jobs rather than sticking to work in the *khat* industry. In any case, at Aweday the estimate for children in the *khat* industry goes up to 50% of the total persons involved[10], and in Wondo Genet it goes up to 70%.[11]

In as much as the subjects of this study are children who are involved in *khat* trade, it is imperative that we assess the age distribution of those children actively participating in local-level *khat* transaction. As discussed in the foregone pages, the argument for a 'work- free childhood' proved to be less watertight and is increasingly on the wane as far as Africa is concerned. The phenomenon of the child worker is not something uncommon in Ethiopia, and is even reported on the rise in recent times owing to the pervasive influence of capitalist elements (such as the cash economy) both in towns and countryside. My empirical evidence is consistent with the original hypothesis that child workers exist and take a major part in the process of *khat* transaction and preparation for market in the *khat* assembling centers of the regions.

The age distribution of those children working in the *khat* industry in the selected sites is worth considering at this juncture, because it is of crucial significance

---

[10] Interview with Abdulhamid Majid (*khat* trader), 12/2/2016, Aweday; and with Abdulhakim Abdulahi (*Warada* Finance office), 14/2/2016, Aweday.

[11] Interview with *Ato* Girma Gobena (Manager of Chuko *Kebele* Administration), 21/12/2015, Chuko; and with Legamo Ledamo (*khat* trader), Chuko, 4/12/2015.

in verifying our claim that children are actively involved in the process of *khat* marketing. Analyzing the situation vis-à-vis the Ethiopian law and other international conventions about working children and their rights would make the discussion more meaningful.

Table 1: Age range of children working in the *khat* industry

Age	Wondo Genet	Aweday	Total
Highest age	18	16	18
Lowest age	8	12	8
Average	14.6	14.3	14.5
SD	2.48	1.09	2.19

Table1 above shows the highest and the lowest age of the sample population confirming that the highest age limit of those involved is 18 years of age while the lowest limit is 8 years, which is a little lower than the age group that is referred to as 'adolescent.' Table 2 below presents the overall age- map of the respondents at the two study sites and plainly shows the pattern of children's involvement in the *khat* industry.

Table 2: Age distribution of the working children

Age	Frequency			% of the working children age in the sample population		
	Wondo Genet	Aweday	Total	Wondo Genet	Aweday	Total
8	3	0	3	3.70%	0.00%	2.7%
9	1	0	1	1.23%	0.00%	0.9%
10	2	0	2	2.47%	0.00%	1.8%
11	6	0	6	7.41%	0.00%	5.4%
12	5	2	7	6.17%	6.67%	6.3%
13	6	6	12	7.41%	20.00%	10.8%
14	6	4	10	7.41%	13.33%	9.0%
15	13	16	29	16.05%	53.33%	26.1%
16	24	2	26	29.63%	6.67%	23.4%
17	11	0	11	13.58%	0.00%	9.9%
18	4	0	4	4.94%	0.00%	3.6%
Total	81	30	111	100%	100%	100.0%

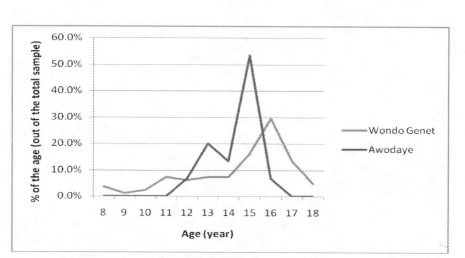

Fig.1: Percentage of age distribution of the working children by research site

Of a particular note here is that the average age of the sample population. As shown on Table 1 above, in Wondo Genet and Aweday it is 14.6 and 14.3 respectively. In spite of the fact that Ethiopia's law, (Proclamation No. 377/2003), establishes the minimum age for employment to be 14, a sizable number of respondents whose ages are below 14 are engaged in work related to *khat* processing and trade; and some of them have already been in the business for more than two years. The graph below (see Figure 1) shows the age/ ages with the highest concentration of respondents. It clearly demonstrates that the majority of children engaged in *khat*- related activities are school-age children, over half of them between the age of 14- 16.

Table 3 below shows that one-third of the sample population of those children involved in *khat* trading activities in Wondo Genet are 'migrants' coming from neighboring *Warada* outside of Wondo Genet. The table also shows the age distribution of both 'migrant' and resident children of the sample population. Of the sample population of the 'migrant' boys 10.3% of them have the lowest minimum age that is just eight. Half of the sample population of the 'migrant' boys are below the minimum working age according to the Ethiopian Labor law, which is 14. In contrast, the highest frequency of working boys among the residents, which is about 78%, is above the age of 15. From this it can be construed that more 'migrant' working children are exposed and vulnerable because they are into the work world at a very young age even below the minimum age required by the law of the country.

Table 3: Resident and 'Migrant' status of the sample population in Wondo Genet

Age	'Migrants'		Residents		Total	
	Frequency	% out of the Migrants	Frequency	% out of the residents	Frequency	% out of the Total
8	3	10.3%	0	0.0%	3	3.7%
9	1	3.4%	0	0.0%	1	1.2%
10	2	6.9%	0	0.0%	2	2.5%
11	3	10.3%	3	5.8%	6	7.4%
12	2	6.9%	3	5.8%	5	6.2%
13	3	10.3%	3	5.8%	6	7.4%
14	4	13.8%	2	3.8%	6	7.4%
15	5	17.2%	8	15.4%	13	16.0%
16	6	20.7%	18	34.6%	24	29.6%
17	0	0.0%	11	21.2%	11	13.6%
18	0	0.0%	4	7.7%	4	4.9%
Total	**29**	**100.0%**	**52**	**100.0%**	**81**	**100.0%**

Unfortunately, for various reasons, we do not have a similar quantitative data helpful to explain the living and working condition of the 'migrant' workers of Aweday thoroughly. Although there are a sizable number of 'migrant' workers in the *khat* industry at Aweday, the fact of the matter is that they did not fill questionnaires. The problem is that; firstly, they do all kinds of work available to them rather than depending on *khat-* related jobs alone. Secondly, most of the 'migrant' workers feel too insecure to tell their 'migrant' status and are resistant to filling questionnaires. Thirdly, they are not distinctly visible as a group and you found them operating individually which makes it difficult to identify who they are. Moreover, asking them where they are from is a 'strange' question that evokes mistrust aggravating their insecurity even farther. Fourthly, the few willing 'migrants' whom I have convinced to fill the questionnaire after an arduous effort, barely reach the required sample size. Thus, I just decided to conduct in-depth interviews with some that are willing to respond to open-ended questions.

3.2   The Work Context for Children in the *Khat* Industry

In this sub- section the study attempts to identify where exactly the labor of the child plays an active role in the *khat* value chain and what distinct works are often performed by children in those centers where *khat* assembling and packing takes place. The following tasks are identified as the domains of the child worker in the *khat* assembling centers. In fact, the labor of the child comes to the picture from the very initial stage of the *khat* value chain, the farm gate. It all starts with pruning and trimming of *khat* leaves and branches to make *khat* bundles ready for transport to the *khat* assembling centers. At Aweday and its environs rarely do traders from towns go to nearby villages to buy the product on the farm. Only few of the *khat* supplying farms to the Aweday market are closely situated to the town of Aweday to be reached by traders from the town to do the harvesting. Those faraway farms known for quality *khat* in most parts of Eastern Hararge send their *khat* to Aweday and this research did not look into the way *khat* is harvested and the labor mobilized and deployed in the process which deserves a special study in its own right.

In the context of Wondo Genet, however, *khat* traders[12] from Chuko town and other neighboring *Warada* which supply *khat* to the *Tafara* market mobilize the labor force for harvesting from among young people around the *khat* farm and its vicinity. Most importantly, however, these traders take the labor to be deployed in the *khat* farms largely from among those 'migrant' boys in Chuko town readily available to take this work. Every morning from 5:00 A.M - 7:00 A.M. more than 200 boys are swarming in the valley of a dry stream at the eastern fringes of Chuko town seeking employment for the day. They are paid on daily basis, and the average amount of pay for these boys may vary from 20-30 birr per day depending on their physical strength and their track record of performance. A few of these boys are also paid in kind. These ones are remunerated by some amount of *khat* leaves collected as a residue while *khat* is cut from trees and when the first- round of trimming and pruning is done at farm-level. This is a low quality *khat* locally known as *pajaro khat* (a Sidama version of Hararge's Tacharo) sold for local consumers in plastic bags. [13]

The other important job open for children is at the market centers where they serve as assistants to traders while they buy *khat* from farmers and other *khat* suppliers. Here, their duty is to select good quality *khat* bundles and to do the

[12] These are specifically traders locally known as *YaGabare- Nagade* ("farmer-trader") who are originally farmers, or at least members of a peasant household, hence farmer-traders. Their principal duty is buying *khat* from farmers on the standing trees and as shrubs on the farms. This in fact is a very demanding duty which requires constant mobility sufficient capital, connection with feeders of information, and bargaining skills.

[13] Interview with Matios Elamo (farmer -trader) and Matios Legede ('migrant' boy), 21/12/2015, Chuko town.

price negotiation on behalf of the *khat* trader (those at the *Tafara* market, whom I call "Agent –Purchasers", and the *Abba Sefera* of the Aweday market) so that farmer- traders agree to the deal proposed by the child's boss. One very important service children at both markets provide is accompanying their respective bosses to the market place and assisting them in the scramble for a better quality *khat*. The role of this group of children in the context of the *Tafara* market is invaluable. This is because of the fact that a good number of the "Agent –Purchasers" operating at the *Tafara* market are non- Sidama traders and need the service of those children both as translators and as middlemen in the price negotiations. At Aweday, children doing this kind of job are known as *Gefeta*. Their major job is bringing as many *khat* suppliers and as much *khat* bundles as possible to their respective client- purchasers in return for a commission payment from the trader. What made the service of the *Gefeta* more desirable to *khat* traders is that they finish the lobbying and the price negotiations on their own.[14]

The other major activity in which the few better skilled children can engage themselves in is probably a highly sophisticated service needed in the "*khat* workshops." The "*khat* workshops" are small and big houses alike situated side by side, or around the *khat* assembling centers. They are platforms where the most decisive operations of 'aggregation' and 're-aggregation,' 'combination' and 'recombination' of different varieties, of *khat* takes place, with the imaginable implications on the retail price. According to a recent study, "It is under the roofs of these small houses that the art of 'playing with form' is practiced with cunning hands well intended to manipulate value" (Girma, 2014). Only the better skilled and experienced children connected to traders might get access to this job. Here children are engaged not simply in wrapping and packing of *khat* bundles, but also in the aggregation and re-aggregation process well intended to maximize profit. This is an important work for both the trader and the children involved. It is important for the trader in that more value is added to the product by just combining and recombining of the same product. For the children, this work is important, as it is the highest paying job in the *khat* industry.

It is interesting to note that the practice is the same at both Aweday and Wondo Genet. In both cases, it is at this level that profit is maximized through manipulation, aggregation and re-aggregation. Children participating in those activities have given different names that are indicative of what exactly is being

---

[14] Interview with Abdulhamid Majid, 12/2/2016, Aweday; Interview with Legamo Ledamo 4/12/2015.

done. In the context of the Wondo Genet market, the variety of activities such as *medereb* (the process of making small wraps) *metefere* and *metqelel* (tying up and wrapping) which are all part of the preparation of smaller units from big bundles, can be put into this category. As widely known among the *khat* trading community at Aweday, the job process concerned with the preparation of smaller units is alternatively known as Zefa or *Shelala*. The major task for those engaged in this work is categorizing *khat* types according to their quality and preparing standard units with varying weights and price tags such as 200 birr, 300 birr, 500 birr 1000 birr etc.[15] This work process is not open to the majority of children in the *khat* industry but only available for those very skilled in the art and trusted by the trader.

The least in the hierarchy of working children in the *khat* industry are those who are engaged in doing the relatively low- paying jobs. These are the porters, the cleaners and the errand boys. The sum total of children engaged in these categories of work comprises the larger majority of children working in the *khat* industry. Secondly, these are tasks that do not require any kind of skill and can be performed by any able-bodied young person; hence they are the least – rewarding jobs. In fact the boundary among these job categories is not that rigid. A child who serves as an errand boy now can be a cleaner after a while, so does a cleaner can run errands whenever the need arises.

The porters are many in number and largely provide their services out of the confines of the "*khat* workshops." Their job usually is to carry big bundles of *khat* from delivery vehicles to the "*khat* workshops," and they assist in the process of measuring the wrapped *khat*. They also fetch the *khat* bundles that passed through the branding, weighing and pricing process to vehicles which take them to their final destinations. The large majority of children engaged in this activity are 'migrant' children coming from neighboring *Waradas* in search of wage employment. Especially in the context of the *Tafara* market, this job is the exclusive domain of the 'migrants'.

The cleaners are those who clean the "*khat* workshops" every now and then at a reasonable interval before the floors of the workshops are swamped by leftovers and *khat* garbage. On the other hand, the area of operation of the errand boys can be anywhere around the *khat* market. They are prominently active at Aweday where their services among others include, buying and bringing cigarettes, soft

---

[15] Interview with Abdulhamid Majid, 12/2/2016, Aweday.

drinks, drinking water, and at times even food for other workers and traders extremely absorbed in their respective duties in the workshops. In general, they provide all the necessary supplies people in the "*khat* workshops" might need any time during the day or at night.

3.3 'Migrant' Children: *Les Misérables* of the *Khat* Industry

The other group of children working in the *khat* industry whose working and living conditions require a separate analysis here is the group, which I refer to as 'migrants'. These are children in their school- ages, the same as the group which I call "residents." However, they do not go to school now. Most importantly these are the most vulnerable and disadvantaged of all the children working in the *khat* industry, hence *Les Misérables.*

Qualitative data demonstrates that 'migrant' children working in the *khat* industry constitute a significant part of the working population both at the Aweday and the Wondo Genet *khat* markets. Coming to the *khat* assembling centers seeking wage employment and unwittingly trapped by that life indefinitely is the hallmark of this group of young boys both at Aweday and Wondo Genet. Those 'migrant' workers at both the two centers have demonstrates that 'migrant' children working in the *khat* industry constitute other commonalities such as very poor living condition and engagement in the most degrading and the least remunerative jobs (such as cleaning and porters). In spite of these commonalities they have also some differences which technically defy a linear analysis treating them as a homogeneous group.

'Migrant' children working in Wondo Genet are different from those working in Aweday. In Wondo Genet, 'migrant' child workers make a cohesive unit that makes them distinct and visible as a group. Places where they sleep at night are distinctly known and are their exclusive quarters. At day break they prowl in groups, both in large and small groups, around the eastern outskirts of Chuko town before heading for the day's work on the farms. And at sundown they repeat the same routine around the *khat* market of Chuko town ready to carry *khat* bundles from the trucks that bring *khat* from the various farms to the inner part of the *khat* market where the stalls are found. The towns people easily identify them partly by their relative shabby dressing and overall appearance, and partly they often are seen together in large or in small groups.

Fig. 2: Field interview with children engaged in *khat* labor in Chuko town

Fig 3: 'Migrant' children and boys waiting for the *khat* job in Chuko town

Fig 4: Very young children in *khat* market in Chuko town

Fig. 5: Young boys working in *khat* workshops in Chuko town

The original home areas of the 'migrant' children swarming around the Tafara market in Wondo Genet are the nearby *Warada* in the Sidama Zone namely; Malaga, Gorche and Shebedino. A few others also mention some far away *Warada* of the same Zone such as Alata-Wondo and Arbegona as places where they have come from. What can be drawn from conversations in group discussion sessions with these participants is that most parents of these children could afford to send their kids to nearby rural schools. The most repeated answer to the same question, why they abandoned their parents' homes and came to Chuko town, is the "changes" they saw on friends and peers who have come to Chuko town earlier and returned back for family visits.

In contrast, the 'migrant' children at Aweday have joined the *khat* industry with a clear purpose of making a living. In fact some of the 'migrant' children interviewed pointed out that they have migrated to the town of Aweday with their fathers who also picked up one or the other kinds of work in the *khat* industry. As the big jobs in the *khat* industry require capital and connection, even the adult 'migrants' are forced to start with low - paying jobs until they are able to penetrate into the oligarchy of senior *khat* traders, or the rank of the *Aba Sefera*. Hopelessness, growing scarcity of arable land and lack of prospects for the agricultural economy in rural areas of East and West Hararge are among the range of push factors for the 'migrant' workers to flock to Aweday seeking employment in the *khat* industry. At least in this case, one cannot totally downplay poverty as a contributing factor.

The education of the 'migrants' and their performance in schools might not be a subject of detailed inquiry because they already are dropouts from the lowest grades of elementary education with only memories of the good old days. Only 9 out of the 29 'migrant' children who filled the questionnaire in Wondo Genet reported that they still go to school confronting the range of adversities and challenges they encounter as "part-time" students. The large majority of 'migrant' children reported that they had been in one of the lowest grades of the first cycle of primary school in their home areas.

Working in the "*khat* workshops" is a much desired and a highly coveted job for this group of children. Getting access to the better types of jobs requires familial ties or some other connections to *khat* traders who run *khat* businesses and own "*khat* workshop." The large majority of those *khat* traders both in Wondo Genet and Aweday are local people, whereas the 'migrants' are "outsiders" with little

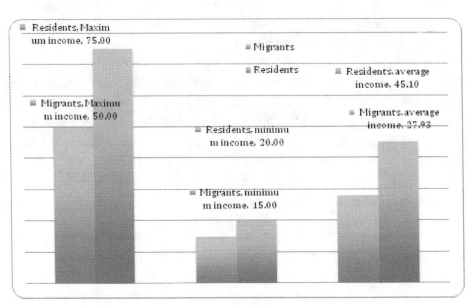

Fig. 6: Daily income of 'migrant' and resident child workers in the *khat* 'industry'

or no chance of having connections to those traders. Therefore, jobs that are open to this group are the contemptible, the most labor intensive and the least remunerative ones. For example, the dominant majority of porters who carry *khat* bundles to and from Isuzu trucks and all around the *khat* markets are 'migrant' children. The result of the survey show that of the total of 29 'migrants', 19 (65.5%) of them get their daily earnings from cleaning and working as porters, while just 5 (9.6%) of the "residents" are engaged in such types of jobs.

Similarly, the daily earnings of the 'migrants' rarely exceed 30 birr a day. There is a higher risk of getting nothing all day long, especially in seasons when the *khat* business itself slows down. Figure 2 above is additional confirmation that the income of the 'migrant' children is indeed by far less than the "resident" children who like them take part in the trading activities of the *khat* industry. The average daily income of the residents is 45.10 birr, while that of the 'migrants' is only 27.93 birr a day. The maximum income of the "residents" as obtained from the sample population goes as high as 75 birr, while that of the 'migrants' does not exceed 50 birr a day.

Their lodgings where they spend the nights are egregiously abominable and perilous. The rooms where they sleep, which for various reasons are impossible

Fig. 7: Young boys carrying heavy load of *khat* to the market (Chuko town)

Fig. 8: Very young children are also engaged in carrying *khat*

Fig. 9: 'Rush hour' at the Tafara *khat* market, Chuko town

Fig.10: Some children engaged in *khat* job while others go to school (Chuko town)

to get access to,[16]are reported to be the worst places for a young person even for a few hours of a night's sleep. Responses are almost unanimous about the number of roommates those rooms accommodate each night. The average number of roommates those 4mt. x 4mt. rooms is reported to be 15-20. Those over-crowded and suffocating rooms by themselves speak volumes about the living conditions of those wretched children of the *khat* industry.

Recently 'migrant' children working in the *khat* industry have become a talking point in Chuko town. Group discussion with local authorities in Wondo Genet reveals that, 'migrant' children have increasingly become a threat to social security. What greatly added to their visibility is not so much their despicable living condition than some reports of virulent communicable diseases that claimed some lives, involvement in criminal activities, and alcohol-driven violence. The most agonizing incident in Wondo Genet that led to a prompt action of local officials was the devouring of one of those children by a hyena while slept in a shack under construction because of his inability to pay for a sleeping place.

Local authorities took the lead to do something about these children. Accordingly, in 2015 it was decided to repatriate 'migrant' children to their home areas. It is not clear where the first instruction for the repatriation of these children came from. But Chuko town's administration was given the mandate to organize the process of repatriation. The number of 'migrant' children to be repatriated was not determined conclusively. According to a local official of Chuko *kebele* Administration, nearly 1,200 'migrant' children (700 in the first round and 500 in second round) were caught and sent back to their home areas. Sadly the deterrent effect of this measure was insignificant and its impact in curbing the flow of 'migrant' children to the town of Chuko was barely minimal.[17]

---

[16] These are shanty places very dismal for visitors. Owners have been repeatedly admonished by local authorities for renting such places and warned not to rent such places any more. But those young children keep on coming every night for they have no other cheaper options than those rented for 3 birr on average per head. By the same token, for owners of those places, the untaxed income of about 60 birr (which is 3x20) every day is no doubt a tempting benefit. For all these reasons owners, I am told, want the milking to continue secretly but do not feel comfortable talking about their "business".

[17] Interview with *Ato* Girma Gobena (Manager of Chuko *Kebele* Administration), 21/12/2015, Chuko town.

This commendable[18] effort to repatriate the 'migrant' children to their original villages was aborted right from the very start. In the words of a local official, "Almost all of those children repatriated were able to come back to Chuko town ahead of the same trucks that carried them to their home areas."[19] It was a hastily arranged endeavor, and failed to bring about a lasting solution to the problem. In the first place, it was a sort of a crisis management to respond to the public uproar created because of the boy devoured by a hyena. A major pitfall was the lack of coordination of officials and other stakeholders involved, and adequate organization of the scheme. Some individuals were even seen providing newly purchased educational materials such as exercise books and pencils to the returnees in the hope of making the process voluntary. Despite all these, the lessons to be learned from the past before embarking on a similar scheme in the future are very important.

3.4   Gender

Last, but not least, to be considered at this juncture is the issue of gender and the division of labor between men and women in the *khat* trading system. In general, as it stands today, in the two *khat* assembling centers, the participation of women in *khat* marketing and trade is marginal. Even more so, "*khat* workshops" are male-dominated places where one can witness a clear gender bias. In large measure, it is this state of affairs that profoundly influenced why much of the discussion and themes raised in this study are male- focused and almost all the respondents are boys.

However, this is not to undermine the enormous capital and riches very few women such as the "big lady of *khat*," Sura Esmael and a lady widely known by the name Qershi have accrued over the years, and the dominant role they play in the *khat* export trade. The former has for long been a trader and *khat* exporter largely to the Somaliland city of Hargessa and other towns in the Ogaden region; while the latter is a notable figure in the *khat* export business to Djibouti. This being said, in Aweday any spectator can see hundreds of women swarming around the *Magala Jimaa* and the main asphalt road heading to Dire Dawa and

---

[18] There was no time to think about a strategically sound solution at that moment. Anything that can halt the rising tension and calm down the public will do for local officials.

[19] Interview with *Ato* Nigatu Girma, (Head, Wondo Genet *Warada* Administration Office), 21/12/2015.

Addis Ababa. Some of these ladies are *Gefeta*[20] and some others are engaged in collecting smaller bundles of *khat* from farmers and putting the smaller fractions together to sell them to traders in kilograms. Still a few others purchase *khat* at Aweday and send it to their business partners in other towns such as Adama and Dire Dawa. But the bottom line is that they are all mature women over 17 and 18 years old. With the exception of a handful of few, the large majority of them are either married women, or widows, or divorcees, and hence not among the target population of this study. Sartu Abdulmelik, a 9th grade student aged 15, whom I was able to interview, is perhaps one of the very few young girls who are taking part in the *khat* trading activities around *Magala Jimaa* and still manage to go to school. Even then, the likes of Sartu are not engaged in activities within the confines of "*khat* workshops."

In Wondo Genet and the *Tafara* market, however, women's participation in *khat* trade has been visibly minimal and only subsidiary. Their role is limited to the provision of *tisho* and *hokkitto* to *khat* traders. In fact *tisho* and *hokkitto* are materials of critical significance without which the process of packaging and wrapping is impossible. *Tisho* is a string made of the fibers of the outer layers of the *enset* trunk. *Hokkitto*, on the other hand, is a local name for the *enset* leaves used for wrapping the larger bundles as well as the several smaller units within the larger bundle. These women traders who specialize in the *tisho* / *hokkitto* business are predominantly married women who are not concerned with their own schooling anymore and rather need the money to supplement their household needs.

3.5   Motivational Factors: Why do Children Work in the *Khat* Industry?

Based on findings from an earlier field work at Wondo Genet, I have been arguing that *khat* trade is a business of the youth (Girma, 2007 E.C.). It absorbs a significant proportion of the youth participating in the *khat* value chain in different capacities. In other words, the youth, more than any other age-group, is a vital force in the process of *khat* transaction at local level. This partly is owing to the very nature of *khat* being a perishable commodity with a shelf life of a maximum of 48 hours. *Khat* maintains its potency if it is used within 48 hours after being

---

[20] As mentioned earlier for boys, this is a gender-free reference that applies to female workers as well who are intermediaries connecting those suppliers who fetch the *khat* from the farm to the market. They make life easier to the client purchase by handling the larger part of the price negotiations on his behalf and get a commission for their service.

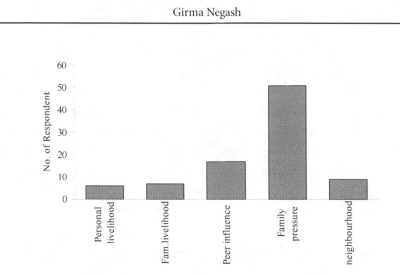

Fig. 11: Reasons for children's participation in *khat* trading activities.

cut. Therefore, *khat* has to be marketed as quickly as possible. That is why the *khat* business requires maximum efficiency and long hours of hard work. Traders and their assistants have to work hard, overcoming fatigue caused by sleepless nights. The business of *khat* trade needs lots of people who can adjust themselves to the urgency and hustle that characterize the trade, and are ready to work under pressure. That is why energetic youth are needed to take up the job of buying, sorting, packing, loading-unloading, transporting, and the selling of *khat* (Girma 2007 E.C: 196-197).

Studies that set out to explore the reasons behind children's involvement in paid labor activities underline poverty as one of the driving factors. It has also been unequivocally pronounced in the *Worst Forms of Child Labor Convention of 1999, No. 182* "… that child labor is to a great extent caused by poverty and that the long-term solution lies in sustained economic growth leading to social progress…." The 1996 "Development and Social Welfare Policy" of the FDRE underlines that 'poverty and marginalization' are major push factors for children to engage in wage employment. For many working children, it is believed, wage employment is either a means of livelihood or a means of supplementing meager family income, or both. However, contrary to this widely held belief, the large majority of children engaged in *khat-* related work in the two study sites are not forced into the *khat* business by a dire need to contribute to the family income. Neither do they consider the income they generate from *khat* business as a lifeline for their families. This is best attested by the responses participants gave to the question why they first went into the *khat* business. As shown in Figure 11 above,

51 out of 90 respondents in Wondo Genet and Aweday, which is 56.67 % of the respondents, replied that they joined the *khat* industry in large measure because of direct and indirect family pressure, however, not so much caused by poverty

Results of in -depth interviews and group discussions adds credence to the assertion that the role of parents, wittingly or unwittingly, pushing their children into the *khat* industry is a factor of an overriding significance. The response of the majority of children to the question why they joined the *khat* industry reveals that there is the hand of parents or a close relative pushing them into the business. A family member, running a *khat* business, is frequently cited as the one reason behind a child's entry into the *khat* industry. Group interviews with the working children in Wondo Genet reveals that, more often than not, the first recruiters of many children into the *khat* industry are either a father, or an elder brother, or an uncle, or one of their cousins. When asked about the reason that enticed them to join the *khat* industry, most working children cite reasons such as; " assisting a father and /or an elder brother already in the business," "to learn the art of the trade from a father, or a brother, or any other relative," " offer from a friend of the father to work in the *khat* industry," " the insistence from one's father/mother to be self- sufficient," "family advice to spend evenings at "meaningful" places than simply wasting time with friends." In sum, these are indicators that poverty and livelihood are less responsible than family pressure in driving children, particularly the 'resident' boys, into working in the *khat* industry in my study localities.

A somewhat intriguing issue that comes to the surface in this connection is that a good number of respondents underlined the fact that parents often insist children, directly or indirectly, to working the *khat* industry. It might sound normal if such parents are of the sort we can call "poor", or who have very little income for family sustenance. But, according to respondents, these are families with average or above average income by local standards. It is also reported that families (with the exception of the very rich ones) in both the two sites encourage children to join the *khat* industry as child workers. The following phrase in Sidama language, has become a daily catchword in several Sidama households when a child is hesitant to take up a job in the *khat* industry; ዜዴሎ ሲአኔ አን,ጋ ኦቲና፤ [literally, "go and work do not see my hands / do not expect from me"]. Some members of the local community are of the opinion that such a family "pressure" is justifiable when seen from the perspective of the responsibility of parents to guide their children to a promising career or a paying job in a region where scarcity of land

39

is a growing problem. The employers prefer young people/children to the rest of the available labor force due to a combination of a number of factors. Firstly, as revealed by the accounts of *khat* traders, who have years of experience employing children in their firms, the major attraction in employing young people/children is relatively cheaper labor cost. Children working in that industry are paid very little as compared to their adult counterparts. A very simple economic truism not hidden to the *khat* trader is that, "If children's productivity is similar to that of adults, the use of child labor is economically rational" (Ansell, 2005: 170). The next attraction that draws the employer towards the labor of children is their speed and efficiency in discharging their duties, an indispensable asset in any firm that runs a *khat* trading business. This in fact proves the view that *khat* trade is the business of the youth. The third important attribute of the labor of the child that attracts employers has more to do with culture than economic imperatives. Employers are often more at ease in giving orders to children and younger people in general than to persons of their own age, or people older than themselves.

3.6   Working in the *Khat* Industry and its Impact on the Child's Education

Children's engagement in Education has been considered as a strong and viable tool in the struggle to mitigate the problem of child labor, or the rising number of working children globally (Education International, 2013:17). A very important instrument adopted by the ILO with the highest relevance to the issue of child labor was the "ILO Convention 138" that solidly establishes access to basic education for all children (EFA) is a key to combat child labor. As stated in the introductory section of this monograph, the purpose of this study is not to explain the correlation between child labor and education *per se*; rather it is intended to shed some light on contexts, such as the one in the *khat* industry, where education and children's work go hand in hand. The findings of this study demonstrate a condition where school-age children are forced to become paid workers in the *khat* industry without a total abandonment of schooling.

It should be established that, the subjects of this study are partly those child workers who combine schooling and working in the thriving *khat* industry of Ethiopia. ILO's reliance on increased access to education as a means of combating child labor has proved to be less of a potent weapon to combat the problem in our case. The situation on the ground in the selected study sites is different in that these children workers are actually enrolled in schools, thus not entirely barred from schooling. The major inquiry in this study is what it is like to be a

40

part-time student, at that early age, allocating much of one's time for something else than education. What are the challenges of the working child that hinder his access to quality education at the right age? Still in the educational sphere, this study attempts to investigate the extent to which this group of children are disadvantaged as compared to the full- time students because of their involvement in an extra- educational activity, *khat* trade. Most importantly, our investigation into their life style and working condition vis-à-vis their performance in school would hopefully unravel the magnitude of the impact working in the *khat* industry has on the education of those children under study. These are the children who I claim are disadvantaged and "victims of socio-economic change." Their right to quality education is slipping out of their hands because they are excessively engrossed by their jobs in the *khat* economy.

Table 4: Working hours

Number of hours they work every night	Wondo Genet		Aweday	
	freq.	%	freq.	%
1 hr	2	2.5%	0	0%
2hrs	4	4.9%	2	6.7%
3hrs	23	28.4%	5	16.7%
4hrs	26	32.1%	5	16.7%
5hrs	14	17.3%	7	23.3%
6hrs	12	14.8%	5	16.7%
7hrs	0	0.0%	4	13.3%
8hrs	0	0.0%	2	6.7%
Total	**81**	**100.0 %**	**30**	**100.0%**

It is demonstrable from the current trend that a good number of children spend a very useful part of their day in an economic activity related to the trade in a stimulant. These children will be subjected to a situation in which they cannot have a balanced and fairly distributed 24 hours. A major causality in this imbalance in the distribution of a child's time is his/her education. Empirical evidence shows that a good number of the school- going children of the *khat* industry are very brave young people determined to pursue their education even under the most unfavorable circumstances. Chief among the challenges is the working hour of the *khat* industry. The working hours of the *khat* industry both at Wondo Genet and Aweday stretch from late afternoon all through the night, and to daybreak as is the case in Aweday. The number of hours individual children are engaged in their daily routine in the *khat* industry may vary from one individual to the other. Table 4 above shows that 32.1% of the respondents in Wondo Genet spend 4 hours every night, and 17.3% spend 5 hours working in the *khat* industry. In Aweday, the figure more or less shows a similar trend. Those who said they spend 4 hours every night are 16.4% of the respondents, while 23.3 % of the respondents spend 5 hours each day and 16.7% said they spend 6 hours every night.

It is crystal clear that these hours are in the night where a child, should go to sleep and get sufficient sleep so that he/she can go to school the next morning. Long working hours in the night might be tolerable when they are for a day or two. But when this is a regular pattern in the life of a child, it is barely possible for such a child to actively follow his/her lessons during the daytime due to the fatigue and exhaustion caused by lack of adequate night's sleep. According to teachers working in local schools of the study areas, fatigue, drowsiness and frequent yawning are some of the signs with which they easily distinguish those who are working in *khat* markets from those who do not. Understandably these are not symptoms of a healthy and motivated child in schools, and more so they are directly proportional to the receptivity and academic performance of those who combine schooling and *khat* trade.

The bottom line here is that it can easily be construed that these circumstances and the overall working condition of those boys in the *khat* industry is by no means in harmony with Article 32 of the Convention on the Rights of the Child (CRC) which reads, "The right of the child to be protected from economic exploitation and from performing any work that is likely to be hazardous or to interfere with the child's education, or to be harmful to the child's health or physical, mental, spiritual, moral or social development." Neither is it the sort of work that can be tolerated as 'less harmful' even by African standards. What reinforces this farther is that the working condition of those children also involves a latent risk on their health not less because of the lack of adequate night's sleep but because of the higher probability of those young boys to picking up a *khat* chewing habit which has the potential of creating addiction.

What emerged from the discussion with FGD participants among those who combine work and schooling is that this group have no time for academic engagements such as studying, going to the library or doing homework in their out- of- school hours. In general, time has always been in short supply for this group of child workers. When they are in the morning shift, the time between lunch hours and the beginning of work in the *khat* markets is too short to concentrate and study unless one has a strong discipline and is time conscious. When they are in the afternoon shift, much of the morning, whether they like it or not, is spent on sleeping. On top of all these, most of them also have family commitments to which they have to contribute their labor in different forms. Other working children outside the *khat* industry may use the night-time for some of those academic activities. On the contrary, the nights are the busy hours of every trader and participant of the *khat* market. It is already stated that even while attending classes these children are suffering from fatigue and drowsiness, which are the consequences of the night-time work in the *khat* markets. These young workers also added that if someone among them tells that he goes to the library even occasionally it must be either a pretentious bravado or one must be a very diligent student with exceptional courage.

Empirical data also suggest that absenteeism is the other chronic problem that hinders the academic performance of children under study. Absenteeism is defined as a regular and unexplained absence of students from school (Brooks, 1997 as cited in Loraine & Ezenne, 2010: 33). A wide range of complex factors might cause absenteeism. It can occur without the knowledge of parents and by some causal factors of the child himself, or herself. It can also occur with the consent of parents as well. Studies have identified two categories of causes of absenteeism. They are family- personal factors and school-related factors. The family- personal category include such factors as low personal and family interest in education, issues related to livelihood, health issues, socio-economic status and geography (location). School-related factors include, among others; boredom with classroom instruction, bullying and peer issues, lack of school support and protection, bad relations with teachers and school authorities, and an irrelevant curriculum. (Loraine &Ezenne, 2010: 33; Gupta & Lata, 2014:13)

The large majority of participants of this study are either in the second cycle of their elementary education, or just 9th grade students. In fact these students, as has been mentioned earlier, are those who combine schooling with work in the *khat* industry. However, the nature of their job, which is demanding, made them miss out some of their school days entirely, or some of their classes each day. Table 5 above shows the response of participants both in Aweday and Wondo Genet to a question whether or not they regularly go to school. They were also asked how many days in a week they miss out if they don't. 73% of the respondents at

Aweday reported that they miss out 1-3 school days a week, whereas 50% of the respondents at Wondo Genet reported that it has become a pattern that they do not to go to school one , or two, or there days a week. In a nutshell, a significant number of the respondents are unable to go to school on a regular basis. Indeed, some of them are absent up to three school- days a week, which means more than 50% of the total number of weekly school days.

Table 5: The rate of absenteeism among those combining work and schooling

No. of days participants miss out classes	Wondo Genet		Aweday	
	Freq.	%	Freq.	%
0 day per week	32	50.0%	8	26.7
1 day/week	10	15.6%	2	6.7
2 days/week	20	31.3%	19	63.3
3days/week	2	3.1%	1	3.3
4days/week	0	0	0	0
TOTAL	64	100.0%	30	100

According to the participants of this study, the major reason for their absence from school is their work in the *khat* industry. They particularly mention the difficulty to wake up in the morning because of sleepless nights as a cause for their absence from school. Once again, we have to note that *khat* markets operate the whole afternoon and the whole night in the case of Aweday, and until late in the night in the case of Wondo Genet. Therefore, it is not a matter of surprise that these children sleep for very few hours in a day. It is also relevant to consider the performance of the child in the class even in those days he has managed to go to school. Although a good number of participants are enrolled in schools, the large majority of them are regular absentees because of the reason stated above. Needless to elaborate that absenteeism is a serious impediment to academic performance and intellectual development of the child.

Missing individual classes, either because of coming late to school or leaving school before the end of classes, is described by experts of the field in a different way. For example G. Bond, in his study *Tackling Student Absenteeism* (2004) refers to this kind of failure to attend classes in full as "fractional truancy." By fractional truancy he meant the condition of students arriving at schools late, or leaving schools early, or missing out individual classes. Both qualitative and quantitative data collected complement each other in showing that the target populations in both the two sites have serious problems in these areas as well. A good proportion of participants are habitual late- comers who are forced to miss the first two or three periods in most days of the week. These same children and a good number of others have the habit of leaving school two or three periods before the end of the day's classes. On the basis of Table 6 below it is demonstrable that only 6.7 % of the respondents at Aweday reported that they are never late to school, whereas 93.3% of them disclosed that they often come to school late. In fact, a total of 86.6% miss out the first two or three periods of the day at least for 2 days a week and at most for 3 days a week. In Wondo Genet the situation seems less severe. "Only" 61% of them come to school late in two, or three, or four days a week. The remaining 39% asserted that they do not have the problem of late- coming.

Table 6: Late - coming

No. of days/week participants come to school	Wondo Genet		Aweday	
	freq.	%	freq.	%
0 day per week	25	39.1%	2	6.7%
1 day per week	12	18.8%	0	0.0%
2 days per week	18	28.1%	13	43.3%
3days per week	8	12.5%	13	43.3%
4days per week	1	1.6%	2	6.7%
Total	64	100%	30	100.0%

The fundamental reason behind habitual late- coming, as far as children working in the *khat* industry are concerned, has an evident linkage with the nature of their job. If one tries to explain the late- coming problem of these specific groups of children with laziness to rise up early and to be at school before class begins, it would be an over simplification of a very complex problem. Group discussion and face-to- face interviews with participants of this study both at Aweday and Wondo Genet are full of complaints about the stressful condition of their work that keeps most of them awake even in post-midnight hours. The persistent struggle of these students working in the *khat* industry to suppress their biological need to sleep for some hours a day is difficult to hide even if one wants to. In one of the high schools in Wondo Genet, the first three periods of the morning shift are the high time of business for the school café crowded with students of the *khat* industry who have to eat their breakfast there. And interestingly, it is neither a punishable wrongdoing nor a reprehensible violation of school regulations.

The other manifestation of the problem of "fractional truancy" is the habit of leaving the school compound earlier than the official end of the school day. The study population, no matter how their numbers in the two study sites might vary, also suffers from this malignant problem. Similarly, the number of days in a week individual participants leave schools earlier might be at variance with one another. As can be evidenced form the figures on Table 7 below, a staggering size of the participants, 90% in Aweday and 71.9% in Wondo Genet, reported that they have the habit of leaving school earlier than the last period, usually at break time.

Table 7: Leaving school early before end of classes

Response to the question "Do you leave school early?"	Wondo Genet		Aweday	
	freq.	%	freq.	%
Yes	46	71.9%	27	90%
No	16	25.0%	3	10%
Unknown	2	3.1%	-	-
Total	64	100%	30	100%

Evidence from varying data sources is suggestive that leaving early from school compounds is a problem for this group of children and its causes are attributable to their participation in the night time *khat* trade. Respondents who have reported that they have this kind of problem pointed out that they do leave schools earlier than the end of the last period, sometimes with the consent of teachers and school officials. Their stated reason is that they have to be present at the *khat* market ahead of time. Although 5:00 pm in the afternoon is the right time for the child worker to get started with his job, respondents believe that in a competitive trading atmosphere the earlier is always the better. This has made the out- of-school flooding of early-leavers to begin earlier in the afternoon, especially after recess time. At Aweday, there seems to be a tacit understanding, between students rushing to the *Magala Jimaa* on the one hand and teachers as well as school officials on the other, about the three periods following the afternoon break.

The prevalence of a high dropout rate among the study population, and its impact on the intellectual development of the group, should have been a subject of thorough analysis, albeit the lack of substantive data that warrants a solid and comprehensive conclusion. Yet we can still rely on sources at hand to make some relevant analysis about the extent of dropping out from school and its impact on the participants of this study. The data obtained from Wondo Genet Secondary and Preparatory School is one such data sources used for this purpose[21]Through computing the numbers from a registration record taken at the beginning of the academic year in September and the roster done at the end of the academic year, we found out that out of 1569 students registered in the academic year 2013/14, only 1,369 sat for the final exam at the end of the year which gives a dropout rate of 200 (12.7%) for that year and that grade level alone.

In the 2014/15 academic year out of 165 students registered at the beginning of the year, only 97 sat for the final exam. In fact the number of new 9th grade students assigned to this school significantly dropped down because of the opening of a new high school in Chuko town and the older one was made to specialize as a preparatory school in the subsequent years. In any case the dropout rate this time is 68 (41.2%) which is higher than the previous year. Nevertheless, this data only helps us to establish the prevalence of students dropping out from school before the end of the academic year. However, this may not warrant a conclusion that the cause behind such a dropout rate is students' participation in *khat* trading activities. But it still is indicative of the prevalence of the problem and the level of its seriousness. Most importantly, however, in as much as some of the students in this school are students working in the *khat* industry, as could be learned from qualitative data, they must have contributed substantively to the rise of the dropout rate. According to FGD participants, the regularity of their attendance, and going to school all- year-round are both at risk because of the seasonality and volatile conditions of the *khat* business.

Overall, students' failure to reach a targeted achievement level, either through premature school leaving [drop-out], or repetition in the same grade, is a failure which authorities of the field aptly call 'educational wastage'(Ekka & Roy, 2014;

---

[21] Grade 9 is the grade in focus and the two academic years we have obtained the data mentioned above are 2013/14 and 2014/15.

L. Pauli, 1971). In broader perspective it indeed is wastage with implications far beyond the local level that has to be reckoned with. It is a failed investment for the nation which provides trained teachers and allocates budget to the school system at large. The following statement is more laconic about the effect and broader implications of the drop-out problems and repeating in the same grade."If a child leaves the school without completing the primary course or it fails in a class, then the investment does not give commensurate returns. As such, both the money and human resources are wasted. This is what we call educational wastage"(Ekka & Roy, 2014:31).

3.7   Threats to the Physical and Mental Well-being of the Child Worker

The dominant theme in the *khat* discourse for a considerable time has been the physical, physiological and psychological harm *khat* chewing is believed to engender (Kennedy, 1987: 214-215; Al-hebshi N. and Skaug, 2005: 303). Although sometimes conflicting with one another, there are research findings with pages of accounts about the deleterious consequences of *khat* chewing. *Khat* researchers within the medical community have done a lot of work in establishing the harmful effects of *khat* on human health. Among the range of diseases and bodily dysfunctions that *khat* is reported to have been a cause for are: gastritis, increased blood pressure, increased respiratory rate, constipation, cancer of the mouth and stomach, loss of teeth, hallucination, illusion, impotence and a lot others (Varisco,2004:104; Dechassa, 2001: 96; Amare & Krikorian,1973:375).

In most studies about *khat* we find the youth in general to occupy the center stage and often mentioned as more vulnerable to picking up *khat* chewing habit in large numbers. A relevant point to cite here is that some researchers even attributed the expansion of *khat* chewing culture among the youth in Ethiopia during the1970s and 1980s to the *Zemecha*-"Campaign for Development through Cooperation, 1975-77- in which high school and college students were the main actors (Ezekiel, 2004: 13). Further than this, recent studies and surveys among High school and college students in Ethiopia reveal that there is a very high prevalence of *khat* chewing habit among the youth with two-thirds of the students in between the ages of 15-22 are frequent users of *khat* (Ezekiel, 2008: 785).

Notwithstanding with some "positive" attributes, the damaging effect of those psychoactive ingredients found in *khat* on the human brain, particularly on the brain of a young person should be noted here owing to its relevance to the broader discussion at hand. Some recent research findings suggest that cases of *khat*-induced psychosis have become more common in Ethiopia and else where. *Khat* may cause a functional psychosis when taken in excess, or by individuals with a history of psychosis problem. It is also reported that a number of chronic *khat* chewers experienced persistent hypnagogic hallucinations or symptoms of schizophrenia-like psychosis (Hassan, N.A.G.M. *et al.*, 2007: 708). A decade earlier, Ethiopian researchers had already established that regular and heavy consumption of *khat* has the potential to complicate the psychiatric conditions of a person (Alem, A., & Shibre, T., 1997:138). What is more alarming here, both as private individuals and as a nation, is the recent epidemiological findings of neuroscience research that concluded the adolescent brain is more vulnerable to the effects of addictive substances than the brain of adults (Lubman*et al.*, 2007: 792).

The target population of this particular study are children in their teens working in the *khat* industry. There are more reasons to believe that their *khat*- related work, their workplace and working conditions might induce in them a *khat* chewing habit. In connection with their role as wage workers, we have tried to examine whether or not a child labor situation prevailed in the process. The other issue of concern elucidated in this study so far has been the extent to which the education of these children has been affected owing to their participation in the process of local- level *khat* marketing and trade. Nonetheless, there is something more: the high likelihood of those children picking up *khat* chewing habit and ultimately turning into regular *khat* chewers. Work in the "*khat* workshops," that makes them spend 6-8 hours a day holding *khat* either on their palms or on their chest all the time, is a fact of life for these children. For a young person of their age as vulnerable and curious as they are, the distance between the chest and the mouth is such a very short one to put the *khat* into the mouth.

In addition to this, "*khat* workshops" are the starting point of the process of *khat* commoditization and incidentally the workplace of these children. They are places stockpiled with an overwhelming quantity of *khat* and the habit of *khat* chewing is not at all a reprehensible behavior among workers therein. Against such background, therefore, it appears reasonable to state the imminent danger those children are exposed to, that is turning into habitual *khat* chewers. One of the prime concerns of this study has been investigating the interface between working in the *khat* industry and being and becoming a habitual *khat* chewer. A two dimensional cause-and effect relationship was anticipated. First the original motif for a child to opt for a job in the *khat* industry might possibly be an already formed *khat* chewing habit. The other alternative is that the child might be attracted to take a job in the *khat* industry for reasons related to subsistence and/ or family livelihood. As the latter is addressed in earlier chapters, I would like to move onto interrogating the data so as to check whether or not their work place environment is capable of influencing these children to become habitual *khat* chewers.

Focus group participant children in Aweday are almost unanimous in expressing their situation that it is in the nature of their job to chew *khat* while working. According to these children, for a worker in the *khat* industry, *khat* chewing is a norm than an exception. Two issues have come out prominently in regard to the reasons why those children are enticed to begin friendship with *khat* and gradually end up habitual *khat* chewers. Firstly, almost everyone in the *khat* industry, irrespective of a person's age, chews *khat* at workplace, and even afterwards. Respondents rather look at each other with astonishment when asked about the specific reasons why they chew *khat*. In short, this implies that *khat* chewing in and around *khat* markets is a normal daily routine regardless of age. The situation is much the same even outside the confines of the *khat* market. The *khat* growing region of East Hararge, Aweday and its environs included, is particularly prone to *khat* chewing. Here *khat* chewing has got cultural endorsement of the community and is even used at social events such as wedding and mourning ceremonies. One can clearly imagine the perception a child who grew in this kind of cultural environment would have towards *khat*.

The second very important reason why people in the *khat* industry, young and old alike, are regular *khat* chewers revolves around the widely held belief that *khat* chewing increases performance and boosts productivity. Scientific research has established that *khat* is a stimulant with psychoactive ingredients, cathinone and cathine (Kalix, 1992). Indigenous knowledge, in *khat* producing areas, seems to have confirmed this and make use of *khat* as a performance enhancer. Studies made in *khat* producing areas reveal that farmers of those areas chew *khat* in the morning with the understanding that *khat* will generate extra energy that would enhance performance in subsequent agricultural activities and ease the hardship of farm labor (Eshetu & H/Mariam, 2001: 104; Anderson, *et al.*, 2007: 4). Hararge is one of those *khat* producing regions where *khat* is believed to have those "positive" attributes, adding to its popularity both among producers and consumers. It should be noted that part of the study group in this research are the products of this culture and this community where *khat* chewing is not morally and religiously reprehensible.

In Wondo Genet, however, the reply of respondents to the question whether or not they chew *khat* at work place is different from the Aweday respondents. In most cases their response to the same question is as short as 'nay.' The number of respondents who have the courage to answer in the affirmative is insignificant. Nevertheless, the reality is different. Other sources sufficiently inform that these children do chew *khat* while working. For example, my own personal observation in the "*khat* workshops" is convincing that for some reason respondents were timid to tell the truth in this case. Although their official answer is "No," a good number of these children chew *khat* at least at their workplace.[22]

A relevant question here is that why these children are so timid in speaking about their *khat* chewing habits. The answer could be sought from the variations in the cultures of the two regions. The dominant majority of the population of East Hararge are followers of Islamic religion where *khat* chewing constitutes a major part in worship practices, during prayers, and celebrations of religious holidays (Ezekiel, 2004, 11).The general picture is that *khat* chewing is not morally reprehensible in these communities. The large majority of the population of Wondo Genet and its environs, however, are Christians belonging to the various Protestant denominations. According to the tradition of the local Protestant Churches *khat* chewing is not only abhorrent but also regarded as a sin. This accounts for the reason why most *khat* farmers as well as local people in the *khat* business barely chew *khat*. Even the few, who do, never do it in public. This is illustrative why my respondents in Wondo Genet are shy to tell the truth about their *khat* chewing habits. In sum, children working in the *khat* industry at both the two study sites, although their number may vary, are exposed to *khat* chewing habits at a tender age because of their involvement and active participation in *khat* marketing and trade. They are therefore exposed to all the physical, physiological and psychological deleterious effects *khat* chewing might cause.

---

[22] This can best be confirmed by the video footage I was able to shoot at the time of my field work. In addition to this, as mentioned above, their teachers recognize those children involved in *khat* trading activities, and more importantly those who are regular *khat* chewers very well. They told me that they do this with relative ease by observing the known symptoms on the faces of this group of children.

4 Conclusion and Recommendations

4.1 Conclusion

The most substantial finding of this study which is consistent with the original hypothesis is that child workers exist and take a major part in the process of *khat* transaction and preparation for market in the two major *khat* assembling centers. The age distribution of those children working in the *khat* industry in the selected sites has also been sorted out which ultimately led us to the conclusion that children below the minimum working age, according to the Ethiopian law and international conventions, are involved. The study also identified where exactly the labor of the child plays an active role in the *khat* value chain and what distinct works children often perform.

The study farther investigated the major reasons for those young boys to be engaged in paid work in the *khat* industry. Accordingly, the study found out that most "resident" boys, with the exception of the 'migrants' both at Aweday and Wondo Genet, are driven to the *khat* industry less by economic factors than by social and cultural reasons. It can be concluded that 'family pressure' or the insistence of parents, or a close relative, directly or indirectly pushing the boy to get into the *khat* business is a crucial reason. A family member, running a *khat* business, is frequently cited as the one reason behind a child's entry into the *khat* industry. The study reveals that the first recruiters of many of the children into the *khat* industry are either a father, or an elder brother, or an uncle, or one of their cousins in the name of assisting the family, or mentoring them in the wisdom of the *khat* business. Nevertheless only a handful of these "resident" children working in the *khat* industry are the sole bread winners of a family and their earnings rarely is a lifeline to the children themselves, or to their families.

The most critical issue in this study is the extent to which children's participation in *khat* trading activities affect their education. The study has explored in what ways did their work in the *khat* industry affect their education. It also examined possible hindrances caused by their engagement in *khat* trading activities that obstruct their academic performance. The following are some of the consequences of being a child worker in the *khat* industry with a direct bearing on the education of the child:

- The result shows that paid work in the *khat* industry, which requires staying very late at night, was a major constraint for those boys. They could not have sufficient time for rest and study, which ultimately incapacitates them to concentrate on their education.

- Those who combine schooling and paid work in the *khat* industry are suffering from fatigue, drowsiness and frequent yawning in classrooms, because of lack of adequate night's sleep, which undoubtedly inhibits their attention and seriously affect their academic performance.

- As hypothesized at the beginning, this study has found out that, their night time job in the *khat* industry greatly contributed to the very high prevalence of absenteeism among the study population.

- A trend observed among those who combine schooling and work in the *khat* industry is the propensity of missing classes and schooldays as a whole. 'Fractional truancy' which is about missing classes, either because of coming late to school or leaving school before the end of classes, best characterizes the school attendance of the target population in both the two study sites. And this study has shown that there is a correlation between the 'Fractional truancy' prevalent among the study population and the nature of their work which regularly keeps them awake in post-midnight hours.

- Qualitative data shows that, especially at the prime time of the *khat* business in the zones of production, which is from November to January when the *khat* business thrives most, a higher attrition rate is reported in the study sites. However, owing to the fact that this is not a controlled study it becomes difficult to tell the rate of attrition among the study population in any precise way. Secondary data regarding attrition obtained from local schools could only help to establish the existence of a correlation between working in the *khat* industry and walkout from school sometime in the middle of the academic year.

As a signatory of ILO's Minimum Age Convention, 1973 (No.138) and Worst Forms of Child Labor, 1999 (No. 182) Ethiopia responded by issuing the 2003 Ethiopian Labor Proclamation (No. 377) that fixed the age of 14 as a minimum age for employment (Art.89, 2). The Labor Law unequivocally prohibited 'young persons' from taking part in any 'hazardous work.' However, the study found out that a significant number of boys below the age of 14 are engaged in paid work in the *khat* industry in different capacities. It is also indicated in this study that the lowest age of those child workers in the two study sites goes as low as 8. Therefore, it can be inferred that what is going on in the *khat* industry is a transgression of the Ethiopian Labor Law. Nevertheless, cognizant of the fact that the issue of child labor is extremely contentious, I decided to refer to those boys participating in the *khat* industry as working children than child labor. Moreover, as a researcher, I have to limit myself to investigate and shade light on a hitherto unknown or under reported situation and be cautious before making allegations that might have serious legal implications.

It also emerged from this study that the target population are very much exposed to picking up the habit of regular *khat* chewing and/or "dependence" at a tender age because of their *khat*- related work, their workplace and working conditions. A more alarming reminder this research would like to underline is that medical research shows that habitual *khat* chewing may eventually cause one or the other type of psychosis; not least the adolescent brain is also reported to be more vulnerable to the effects of addictive substances than the brain of adults.

4.2   Recommendations: Imagining a Better Future

The study has examined the state of children's involvement in *khat* trading networks both in Eastern and Southern Ethiopia. It has shown the imminence of a major threat posed by the on-going *khat* trading practices. We tried to bring aspects of the trading practices and the role of children in the *khat* value chain to the lime light in the hope that authorities Civil Society Organizations, parents and the public at large will make sense of what is going on around them and act towards the mitigation of the problem.

The following are some feasible actions largely aimed at mitigating the problem in a situation where complete ban of the child's involvement in paid work is not possible. Two major approaches deem to be quintessential in guiding the wide variety of actions to be implemented. They are sensitization of local communities about the *khat*-born danger on children and local youth; and ways of introducing necessary regulatory measures.

4.3 Sensitization and Awareness Creation

In as much as family pressure proved to be the dominant factor in driving children into working in the *khat* industry it is imperative that parents have a stake and should play a fundamentally critical role in dealing with the problem. Therefore, series of platforms aimed at making thorough deliberations, brainstorming and educating local level stakeholders that these boys are working in the *khat* industry risking their health, their education, and overall intellectual development, are necessary.

Such platforms must engage other local level stakeholders such as *Warada* officials, education bureau officials, *khat* traders, farmers, teachers etc.

Apart from the above-mentioned local actors, Civil Society Organizations working at national and local level should play a very active role in the whole process and work in partnership with local stakeholders from organizing those platforms to the execution of the intended programs of educating the public.

All the above stakeholders, especially *Warada* officials and parent must be sensitized that the right to education is a fundamental constitutional and universal right for the child. Article 28 and 32 of the United Nations "Convention on the Rights of the Child" (CRC), which Ethiopia ratified on 9 December 1991 should be considered relevant. Articles 28(1) specify detailed obligations imposed upon states and parties committed that free education at the primary level is a **core minimum** all countries must fulfill. Article 36 of the FDRE constitution not only recognizes the right of the child to education but also prohibits employment which may be hazardous or harmful to the education of the child. Therefore, this should be known to all that it is the responsibility of the Ethiopian government as well as parents themselves to guarantee each child's right to an education.

Although more research is needed, the results from this one do suggest that employment at a very young age may have lasting adverse effect/s on adult health, and that this should be taken into account in the debate about how best to address the issue of child labor. Given the fact that the age of 14 is the minimum age limit set by the labor law of Ethiopia, awareness needs to be created in those *khat* trading localities about this particular provision and the health hazards intrinsic to the nature of the job theses children are involved.

In the short term, authorities in education bureau, or local schools should be sensitized that drop-out problems, absenteeism and repeating in the same grade are all educational wastages that profoundly affect the efficiency of the educational system at large.

We also propose organizing 'action weeks' where by parents, government authorities, Civic Society Organizations and education bureau officials and all other stakeholders meet to deliberate and share ideas on the above-mentioned issues about the education of children, and none other than that, as a good strategy that would allow a focused discussion and add urgency to the matter.

4.3.1 Regulatory Measures

Strict observance of the minimum age limit: Proposing a policy response about child labor or working children is more difficult. For one thing many families depend on the labor of their children as a means of livelihood. Although it is less so in the case of our study sites, the contribution of children's earnings to household income is important in many developing countries. As has been exhaustively discussed in the theoretical part of this study, many African cultures consider children's work as a mode of social integration, and children should not be disengaged from participation in both consumption and production. Therefore, prohibiting children's participation in the informal or the formal sector, or abruptly banning child labor from the economy, would not be a feasible solution to the problem of child labor. But there still is the possibility of putting in place some sort of regulatory scheme, the most crucial of which will be **strict observance of the minimum age limit**, or even renegotiate for a new one if 14 is considered big.

Against this background, authorities at Regional and Zone level, and other responsible government official need to devise a legal framework governing the age-limit of children engaged in *khat* marketing activities, and follow up its actual enforcement

This study indisputably established that a sizable number of children working in the *khat* industry are 'migrants' coming from faraway places to reside and work in those *khat* assembling centers. Repatriation of 'migrant' children to their locality of origin is an option to address the current crises of rising crime rate and deaths from curable diseases caused by poor sanitation and malnutrition. In the long run too, it helps to reduce the number of 'migrants' in those towns and discourage newcomers. But implementation should learn from past experiences and failures. An earlier effort to repatriate these 'migrants' to their place of family origin failed to achieve the desired end because of lack of coordination of stakeholders and efficient organization. Lessons must be learned from the past before embarking on a future endeavor.

A key consideration for Civil Society Organizations and government institutions before a future repatriation scheme is to make the process **voluntary**. The use of force in a repatriation process will be a detriment than a guarantee for success. A key to such a project would therefore be lobbying and convincing the will– be- returnees beforehand.

The marketing system of any product, whether agricultural or industrial, is an important element in the production equation. It is evident that the existing *khat* marketing system has given rise to the involvement of under- aged children in the *khat* industry. By doing so it exposed them to exploitation and numerable other health risks at their tender age. In fact, on previous forums where the issue of *khat* was discussed the absence of a policy framework governing the production and marketing of *khat* was emphasized. We are now at the point where there should not be any procrastination to revisit and overhaul the existing *khat* marketing system in such a way that it benefits both the economy and society.

It is shown that the expansion of schools failed to be a counter check to the rising number of working children, at least as an alternative option we have to consider and think about designing school systems compatible to the working condition and the needs of the children of concern here than pressing them to abandon either school or paid work, which appears to be a difficult choice.

References

Abebe, T. & Kjørholt, A.T. (2009) Social Actors and Victims of Exploitation: Working Children in the Cash Economy of Ethiopia's South. *Childhood*, 16: 175-194.

Al-hebshi N. and Skaug N (2005) *Khat (Catha edulis)* - An Updated Review *Addiction Biology* (2005) 10: 299-307.

Amare Getahun and Krikorian A.D. (1973) "Chat: Coffee's Rival From Harar, Ethiopia I. Botany, Cultivation and Use." In *Economic Botany*. 27 (4): 353-389.

Anderson, D., Beckerleg, S., Hailu, D., Klein, A., (2007) The Khat Controversy: Stimulating the Debate on Drugs. Oxford, New York: Berg.

Ansell, Nicola (2005) *Children ,Youth and Development.* London: Routledge.

Assefa Bquele and Boyden, Jo. (1988) 'Child Labor: Problems, Policies and Programmes,' in Assefa, B, and Boyden, J. (eds.) *Combating Child Labor*, Geneva: International Labor Office.

Alem, A., &Shibre, T. (1997) *Khat* induced psychosis and its medico-legal implication: A case report. *Ethiopian Medical Journal,35*(2), 137-141.

Beckerleg, Susan. (2006) "What Harm? Kenyan and Ugandan Perspectives on *Khat*." *African Affairs*, 105/419: 219–241.

Bourdillon, M.(ed.) (2000) *Earning a Life: Working Children in Zimbabwe.* Harare: Weaver Press.

_____ (2006) *Child Domestic Workers in Zimbabwe*. Harare: Weaver Press.

Bourdillon, M. and Boyden, J. (2014) "Introduction: Child Poverty and the Centrality of Schooling." In Bourdillon, M. and Boyden, J.(eds.) *Growing Up in Poverty: Findings from Young Lives.* Hampshire: Palgrave & Macmillan: 1-19.

Creswell, John. (2003) *Research Design: Qualitative, Quantitative & Mixed Methods Approach* (2nd ed.). SAGE Publications, Inc. Thousand Oaks.

CSA. Population and Housing Census of Ethiopia (2007) Statistical Report for SNNPR:

Education International. (2013) "Child Labor and Education for All: A Resource Guide for Trade Unions and a Call Against Child Labor and Education for All."

Ekka, Rajesh & Roy, Prohlad (2014) "Educational Wastage: A Problem of Primary Education." *American International Journal of Research in Humanities, Arts and Social Sciences.*14-117: 31-34.

Eshetu Mulatu and Habtemariam Kassa (2001) "Evolution of Small Holder Mixed Farming Systems in the Harar Highlands of Ethiopia: The Shift Towards Trees and Shrubs," in *Journal of Sustainable Agriculture*. 18 (4) :81-109.

Ezekiel Gebissa (2004) *Leaf of Allah: Khat and Agricultural Transformation in Hararge, Ethiopia 1875-1991*. London: James Currey.

_____ (2008) "Scourge of Life or an Economic Lifeline? Public Discourse on Khat (*Catha edulis*) in Ethiopia."In *Subsistence Use and Misuse*. Vol. 43 :784- 802.

Gessesse Dessie (2007) *Forest Decline in South Central Ethiopia : Extent, History and Process.* Stockholm, Department of Physical Geography, Doctoral Dissertation.

Girma Negash (2014) "Agriculture and Trade in Northern Sidama Since 1950: A History." PhD Dissertation in History, AAU.

_____ (2007 E.C.) "ጫት መጣቶችና ሥራአጥነት An article in an Amharic language publication by Forum for Social Studies (FSS) titled መጣትና ልማት በኢትዮጵያ

Green, R. H. (1999) "*Khat* and the Realities of Somalis: Historic, Social, Household, Political and Economic." *Review of African Political Economy No.* 79: 33–49.

Gupta, M. & Lata, P. (2014) "Absenteeism in Schools: A Chronic Problem in the Present Time" *Educationia Confab*3 (1): 11-16.

Hassan, N.A.G.M., Gunaid, A.A., Murray-Lyon, I.M. (2007) "Khat (Catha edulis): Health Aspects of khat Chewing." Eastern Mediterranean Health Journal 13(3): 706-718.

Johnson, B., Onwuegbuzie, A., Turner, L. (2007) "Toward a Definition of Mixed Methods Research." Journal of Mixed Methods Research, Vol. 1(2) : 112-133.

Kalix Peter (1992) Cathinone, a Natural Amphetamine. *Pharmacological Toxicology* 70(2):77-86.

Kjørholt, A.T. (2004). "Childhood as a Social and Symbolic Space: Discourses on Children as Social Participants in Society."PhD Dissertation, Department of Education / Norwegian Center for Child Research.

Kassouf, A.L., McKee, M. and Mossialos, E. (2001) 'Early Entrance to the Job Market and its Effect on Adult Health: Evidence from Brazil', *Health Policy and Planning*, 16: 21–28.

Katz, Cindi (2004) *Growing up Global*. Minneapolis: The University of Minnesota Press.

Kennedy, John G. (1987) *The Flower of Paradise: The Institutionalized Use of the Drug Qat in North Yemen*. Dordrecht: D. Reidel Publishing Comp.

Loraine *D.* Cook and Austin Ezenne (2010) "Factors Influencing Students' Absenteeism in Primary Schools in Jamaica, Perspectives of Community Members," *Caribbean Curriculum* Vol. 17: 33-57.

Lubman, D.I., Yucel,M., Hall,W.D. (2007) "Substance Use and the Adolescent Brain: A Toxic Combination." In Journal of Psychopharmacology 21(8): 792-794.

Nieuwenhuys, O. (1998) 'The Paradox of Child Labor and Anthropology', *Annual Review of Anthropology* 25: 237–51.

Nsamenang, A.B. (2008) "Agency in Early Childhood Learning and Development in Cameroon."*Contemporary Issues in Early Childhood* Volume 9 (3): 211-223.

Pauli. L (1971) "Wastage in Education, a World Problem: A Study Prepared for the International Bureau of School of Education." University of Bristol (United Kingdom) and UNESCO: IBE Paris- Geneva.

Tizita Abate (2010) "Children's Everyday Life and Local Market: The Case of Children in Cash Crop Context in Southern Ethiopia."M.A. Thesis in Childhood Studies, Trondheim.

Varisco, D.M. (2004) "The Elixir of life or the Devil's Cud? The Debate over Qat (*catha edulis*) in Yemeni Culture," in R. Coomber *et al* (eds.), *Drug Use and Cultural Contexts: Beyond the West*. London: Free Association Books: 101-118.

World Health Organization (2006) WHO Expert Committee on Drug Dependence 34th Report: Report Series 942. Geneva, Switzerland.

Yeshigeta Gelaw, Abraham Haile-Amlak (2004) *"Khat* Chewing and its Socio-Demographic Correlates among the Staff of Jimma University" *Ethiopian Journal of Health Development* 18(3): 179-184.

Unpublished Materials

Aweday Town Administration (2014) A brochure titled "The Foundation of Aweday and its Overall Features" Aweday Town Administration (2015). A brochure titled" Come and Invest in Aweday."

Dechassa Lemessa (2001) *"Khat (Catha edulis*): Botany, Distribution, Cultivation Usage and Economics." Un- Emergencies Unit for Ethiopia. Addis Ababa.

Kingele, Ralph (1998) "Hararghe's Farmers on the Cross-Roads Between Subsistence and Cash Economy" Unpublished UN document by UN Emergency Unity for Ethiopia."

Sidama Zone Administration (2004 E.C.) Socio- Economic Profile, 2004 E.C. Hawasa, Ethiopia.

News Papers, Proclamations & International Conventions

Ethiopian Herald, "Sell not Serve, What Does it Mean?" Vol. LXVI (198), 29 April 2010. Proclamation No.1/195, Constitution of the Federal Democratic Republic of Ethiopia Proclamation No. 213/2000, The Revised Family Code of the Federal Democratic Republic of Ethiopia.

Proclamation No.414/2004, The Criminal Code of the Federal Democratic Republic of Ethiopia Proclamation No. 377/2003, Labor Proclamation

International Labor Organization. (1973) Minimum Age Convention, No.138.

International Labor Organization. (1999) Worst Forms of Child Labor, No. 182

Sources from the Web

Bond, G. (2004) Tackling Student Absenteeism: Research Findings and Recommendations for School and Local Communities. Retrieved http://www.hwllen.com.au/Text/1062829817063-3396/uploaded Files/ 1112325248500-2929.doc.

Ghetnet Metiku (2010) Study on Child Labor in Ethiopia: An Assessment of the National Policy and Legislative Response to Child Labor in Ethiopia. Online document retrievedon March 10,2016.

Government of the Netherlands, Ministry of Immigration, Integration and Asylum; Ministry of Health Welfare and Sports; and Ministry of Security and Justice, "Ban on *Khat*," 10 January 2012 Accessed on 29/04/2017 from http://www.government. News/2012/01/10/ban-on-*Khat*.html

United Nations (1989) "Convention on the Rights of the Child" (CRC), Accessed onhttp://www.unicef.org/crc/crc.htm.

Printed in the United States
By Bookmasters